AMERICAN
WAR LIBRARY

★ The Iraq War ★

WEAPONS OF WAR

AMERICAN
WAR LIBRARY

★ The Iraq War ★

WEAPONS OF WAR

Titles in the American War Library series include:

The Iraq War
The Homefront
Life of an American Soldier in Iraq
Rebuilding Iraq
Weapons of War

The American Revolution

The Civil War

The Cold War

The Korean War

The Persian Gulf War

The Vietnam War

The War on Terrorism

World War I

World War II

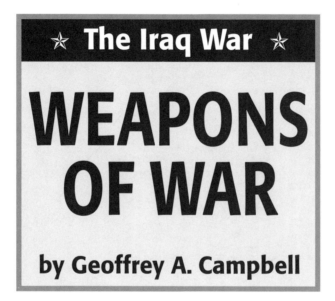

The Iraq War

WEAPONS OF WAR

by Geoffrey A. Campbell

LUCENT BOOKS

An imprint of Thomson Gale, a part of The Thomson Corporation

THOMSON

GALE

Detroit • New York • San Francisco • San Diego • New Haven, Conn. • Waterville, Maine • London • Munich

Dedication: To Mackenzie, Kirby, Nick, and all children, that they may live in a world without war.

For more information, contact
Lucent Books
27500 Drake Rd.
Farmington Hills, MI 48331-3535
Or you can visit our Internet site at http://www.gale.com

LIBRARY OF CONGRESS CATALOGING-IN-PUBLICATION DATA

Campbell, Geoffrey A.
    Weapons of war / by Geoffrey A. Campbell.
        p. cm. — (American war library. Iraq War)
    Includes bibliographical references and index.
    ISBN 1-59018-544-7 (hardcover : alk. paper)
    1. United States—Armed Forces—Weapons systems. 2. Military weapons—United States—History—21st century. 3. Iraq War, 2003—Equipment and supplies. I. Title. II. Series.
    UF503.C36 2004
    956.7044'34—dc22
                                                            2004010318

Printed in the United States of America

★ Contents ★

Foreword 9

Introduction: "Iraq Has Stockpiles of . . . Chemical . . . Agent" . 11

Chapter 1: Naval Assets: Fire, and Comfort, from the Sea . . . 14

Chapter 2: Aircraft over Iraq: The Fixed-Wing Arsenal 25

Chapter 3: Helicopters in Iraq: "If They Move,

      We'll Go After Them" 36

Chapter 4: Fire from the Air: Shock and Awe 46

Chapter 5: Ground War Weapons: "The Baghdad Urban

      Renewal Project" 57

Chapter 6: Surveillance 67

Chapter 7: Psychological Operations: "Your Cause Is Lost" . . 77

Chapter 8: The Limits of Technological Superiority 87

Notes 97

For Further Reading 100

Works Consulted 101

Index 104

Picture Credits 111

About the Author 112

A Nation Forged by War

The United States, like many nations, was forged and defined by war. Despite Benjamin Franklin's opinion that "There never was a good war or a bad peace," the United States owes its very existence to the War of Independence, one to which Franklin wholeheartedly subscribed. The country forged by war in 1776 was tempered and made stronger by the Civil War in the 1860s.

The Texas Revolution, the Mexican-American War, and the Spanish-American War expanded the country's borders and gave it overseas possessions. These wars made the United States a world power, but this status came with a price, as the nation became a key but reluctant player in both World War I and World War II.

Each successive war further defined the country's role on the world stage. Following World War II, U.S. foreign policy redefined itself to focus on the role of defender, not only of the freedom of its own citizens, but also of the freedom of people everywhere. During the Cold War that followed World War II until the collapse of the Soviet Union, defending the world meant fighting communism. This goal, manifested in the Korean and Vietnam conflicts, proved elusive, and soured the American public on its achievability. As the United States emerged as the world's sole superpower, American foreign policy has been guided less by national interest and more by protecting international human rights. But as involvement in Somalia and Kosovo prove, this goal has been equally elusive.

As a result, the country's view of itself changed. Bolstered by victories in World Wars I and II, Americans first relished the role of protector. But, as war followed war in a seemingly endless procession, Americans began to doubt their leaders, their motives, and themselves. The Vietnam War especially caused the American public to question the validity of sending its young people to die in places where they were not particularly wanted and for people who did not seem especially grateful.

While the most obvious changes brought about by America's wars have been geopolitical in nature, many other aspects of society have been touched. War often does not bring about change directly, but acts instead like the catalyst in a chemical reaction, accelerating changes already in progress.

Some of these changes have been societal. The role of women in the United States had been slowly changing, but World War II put thousands into the workforce and into uniform. They might have gone back to being housewives after the war, but equality, once experienced, would not be forgotten.

Likewise, wars have accelerated technological change. The necessity for faster airplanes and more destructive bombs led to the development of jet planes and nuclear energy. Artificial fibers developed for parachutes in the 1940s were used in clothing of the 1950s.

Lucent Books' American War Library covers key wars in the development of the nation. Each war is covered in several volumes, to allow for more detail and context, and to provide volumes on often neglected subjects, such as the kamikazes of World War II, or the weapons used in the Civil War. As with all Lucent books, notes, annotated bibliographies, and appendixes such as glossaries give students a launching point for further research. In addition, sidebars and archival photographs enhance the text. Together, each volume in The American War Library will aid students in understanding how America's wars have shaped and changed its politics, economics, and society.

"Iraq Has Stockpiles of . . . Chemical . . . Agent"

F ollowing the terrorist attacks on September 11, 2001, the United States initiated a bold strategy of proactively seeking out terrorist groups and the countries that harbored them. In late 2001 the United States launched a war against terrorism with the invasion of Afghanistan to dismantle the al Qaeda terrorist organization, which had been responsible for the September 11 attacks, and the Taliban regime that harbored it. Once the Taliban had been run from power, the United States looked elsewhere in the Middle East for significant potential terrorist threats to U.S. security.

The government's attention quickly turned to Iraq, long ruled by the despotic and cruel Saddam Hussein. Based on what they claimed was accurate intelligence, President George W. Bush and high officials in his administration accused Hussein of possessing enormous stocks of so-called weapons of mass destruction, a category that includes not only nuclear weapons but also chemical and biological poisons capable of inflicting widespread death and destruction. Appearing on the television news program *Face the Nation*, Defense Secretary Donald Rumsfeld said on March 23, 2003, "We have seen intelligence over many months that they have chemical and biological weapons, and that they have dispersed them and that they're weaponized and that, in one case at least, the command and control arrangements have been established."[1] The U.S. government had previously claimed that Iraq was on the verge of acquiring or manufacturing nuclear weapons. In an October 7, 2002, speech in Cincinnati, Bush asserted, "The evidence indicates that Iraq is reconstituting its nuclear weapons program. . . . Iraq has attempted to purchase high-strength aluminum tubes and other equipment needed for gas centrifuges, which are used to enrich uranium for nuclear weapons."[2] The Bush administration maintained that Hussein had links to terrorist organizations and that therefore these weapons could be used not only for Hussein's own dangerous purposes but also by terrorist groups intent on harming the United States.

In a series of high-profile presentations to the United Nations, the administration sought to build an international case for war against Iraq. Others in the international community, however, were not so certain. They believed that thorough independent inspections should be continued in order to ascertain whether Iraq indeed had produced prohibited weapons. The administration countered that exhaustive inspections had gone on long enough because its intelligence reports showed that Iraq did, in fact, possess weapons of mass destruction. In one presentation to the United Nations, U.S. secretary of state Colin Powell said, "Our conservative estimate is that Iraq has stockpiles of between 100 and 500 tons of chemical weapons agent . . . enough to fill 16,000 battlefield rockets."[3]

Although opposition to an invasion of Iraq was widespread in the international community, including traditional allies such as France and Germany, the United States decided to make a preemptive strike against Iraq to prevent Hussein from using or sharing his weapons of mass destruction. President Bush also justified the war, code-named Operation Iraqi Freedom, as a means of removing a brutal dictator from power and a step toward building a foothold for democratic rule in the conflict-ridden Middle East. Thirty-four other countries, primarily Great Britain, ultimately committed funds, supplies, or small contingents of troops to a military coalition to invade Iraq, but Operation Iraqi Freedom was overwhelmingly U.S. led and manned.

The Iraq War would prove to be a much different war than that waged by a much stronger allied coalition in the 1991 Operation Desert Storm. In that first Gulf War, the U.S.-led coalition relied on overwhelming force to drive Iraq from Kuwait. In Operation Iraqi Freedom, however, the United States used a much smaller force, utilizing a stunningly sophisticated array of high-technology weapons to drive Hussein from

On May 1, 2003, President Bush declares the end of combat operations in Iraq.

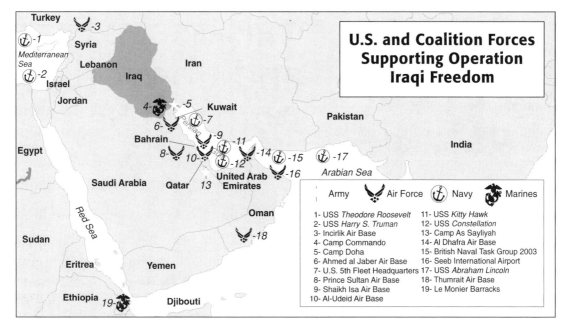

U.S. and Coalition Forces Supporting Operation Iraqi Freedom

Army   Air Force   Navy   Marines

1- USS *Theodore Roosevelt*   11- USS *Kitty Hawk*
2- USS *Harry S. Truman*   12- USS *Constellation*
3- Incirlik Air Base   13- Camp As Sayliyah
4- Camp Commando   14- Al Dhafra Air Base
5- Camp Doha   15- British Naval Task Group 2003
6- Ahmed al Jaber Air Base   16- Seeb International Airport
7- U.S. 5th Fleet Headquarters   17- USS *Abraham Lincoln*
8- Prince Sultan Air Base   18- Thumrait Air Base
9- Shaikh Isa Air Base   19- Le Monier Barracks
10- Al-Udeid Air Base

power. The use of so-called smart weapons allowed the military to achieve its objectives with minimal collateral damage, fewer troops, and a relatively small number of casualties given the scope of the operation.

These weapons were used with enormous effect to rout the Iraqi military and topple the government. At the same time, they preserved essential infrastructure and minimized civilian casualties. Fielding the most technologically advanced military ever assembled, the U.S.-led coalition achieved these goals in far less time than the much larger U.S. force took to achieve its goals in Operation Desert Storm. As Bush said on May 1, 2003, when he declared the military phase of the Iraq War over:

Operation Iraqi Freedom was carried out with a combination of precision and speed and boldness the enemy did not expect, and the world had not seen before. From distant bases or ships at sea, we sent planes and missiles that could destroy an enemy division, or strike a single bunker. Marines and soldiers charged to Baghdad across 350 miles of hostile ground, in one of the swiftest advances of heavy arms in history. You have shown the world the skill and the might of the American Armed Forces.[4]

The weapons demonstrated that the United States remained the world's preeminent military power. However, the conflict also showed the limits of technology and the difficulty of using even the most sophisticated weapons against what threatened to become a war of insurgency and asymmetric tactics.

Chapter 1

Naval Assets: Fire, and Comfort, from the Sea

T he Iraqi navy, never a major military force, had been decimated by coalition forces during the Persian Gulf War in 1991. Never credibly rebuilt following that conflict, the Iraqi navy posed no threat to U.S. and allied forces in the Iraq War. Though Iraq had no credible naval force, however, the United States deployed its navy in the Iraq War to ensure the safety of soldiers and machinery and add flexibility and lethal power to the U.S. assault.

Moving War Matériel

From a purely practical standpoint, the U.S. military had to rely on the navy to get vast supplies of heavy equipment halfway around the world to Iraq. Waging war in the Middle East presented military officials with a major logistical challenge: how to move tons of war matériel to a battle zone far from U.S. supply bases. Military planners had long recognized the need to be able to get equipment to hot spots around the world quickly, so the U.S. Navy was already equipped with

what are called maritime prepositioning ships. Each of the navy's sixteen prepositioning ships are preloaded with enough equipment, supplies, and ammunition to support a U.S. Marine Corps force of seventeen thousand personnel for a month. Twelve such ships were used in direct support of the Iraq War in 2003.

Following the 1991 Gulf War, the military recognized that, although its prepositioning ships could move matériel to hot spots quickly for short durations, a greater sealift capability was needed to get more machinery to a troubled region for extended operations. After extensive study, the military developed what it rather ineloquently called large, medium-speed roll-on/roll-off ships. These ships have the capacity to carry a complete U.S. Army task force consisting of fifty-eight tanks, forty-eight Bradley vehicles, and nine hundred trucks and other wheeled vehicles. In addition, the ships have 380,000 square feet of cargo-carrying capacity, an amount roughly equal to eight football fields. The ships are designed with ramps to facilitate moving vehicles on and off the ship, and two cranes on the ship help expedite loading and unloading of cargo when facilities onshore are inadequate.

While the large ships are capable of bringing vast amounts of equipment to a troubled region, military planners also identified the need for faster cargo ships. The navy's aptly named fast-sealift ships travel at speeds of up to thirty-three knots and can sail from the east coast of the United States to the Persian Gulf in eighteen days. These ships are billed by the navy as the fastest cargo ships ever constructed. Originally developed for commercial use, the ships' high fuel consumption made them unsuitable for merchant marine use. The navy began buying the ships in 1981. Its current fleet of eight fast-sealift ships can carry 90 percent of an entire U.S. Army mechanized division.

The ships are especially useful in rapidly transporting bulky machines such as tanks, large wheeled vehicles, and helicopters across the globe. During and after the Iraq War, fast-sealift ships moved 13 percent of all military cargo.

Cargo ships played an integral role in Operation Iraqi Freedom. Together, the large, medium-speed roll-on/roll-off and fast-sealift ships hauled more than 90 percent of all the combat gear and supplies used during the war, and they continued bringing needed supplies during the year-long reconstruction period after May 2003. As one measure of how large a role the ships played in the war effort, roughly 120 military cargo ships are in active use at any one time during normal peacetime operations around the globe. At the height of the war, however, 167 of the fleet's 214 cargo ships were on active duty solely to support the Iraq

Cargo Ships

The advanced technology and overwhelming firepower of the U.S. Army was instrumental in helping bring about a quick end to Operation Iraqi Freedom. The army's gear, however, is intended for use on land, and without the U.S. Navy, the army would not have played a role in the war at all.

The navy's large cargo ships helped to ensure that the army got its heavy equipment and its supplies. Utilizing large, medium-speed roll-on/roll-off ships (LMSR), the navy made sure the army was equipped with its Humvees, trucks, heavy combat equipment, fuel, and ammunition.

Even after combat operations were officially declared over by President George W. Bush, the navy's Military Sealift Command remained busy. In August 2003, for example, the U.S. Army's Eighty-second Airborne Division deployed to Iraq to replace the army's Third Infantry Division. The replacement required the navy to ship hundreds of thousands of square feet of the Eighty-second Airborne Division's combat equipment. The delivery strained the capacity of three LMSR ships: the USNS *Dahl,* USNS *Soderman,* and USNS *Seay.*

The Military Sealift Command was the primary unit responsible for ensuring that combat equipment got to Iraq. In any foreign war, most military equipment is sent by sea because it is the only practical way of moving vast amounts of cargo quickly and efficiently.

War effort. One hundred and twenty-seven of the ships carried combat equipment and cargo from the United States and Europe.

Mine-Clearing Operations

The Iraqi navy had no such strength. Iraq had one missile-equipped fast-attack craft and one large patrol craft at its disposal, hardly a significant threat to the naval might assembled by the United States, United Kingdom, and other allies in the region. Moreover, coalition planners correctly suspected that the ships Iraq had on hand were of questionable use and readiness. However, although Iraq could not hope to compete in a ship-to-ship battle, allied forces were well aware that Iraqi forces could wreak havoc with so-called asymmetric attacks. For example, through the use of mines seeded throughout waterways and ports, Iraqi troops and government sympathizers could inflict significant damage to the high-technology ships of the U.S. Navy. In the Persian Gulf conflict twelve years before, the only significant damage Iraq was able to inflict against U.S. ships came through the use of mines, which severely damaged the USS *Tripoli* and the USS *Princeton*. Consequently, the navy devoted significant resources to ridding the region of floating, moored, and seabed mines.

One of the most significant mining-clearing efforts of the Iraq War took place in Umm Qasr, Iraq's only deepwater port. Securing the port, and ridding it of mines, was of crucial importance to the war effort. Coalition forces wanted to control the port

as soon as possible to provide matériel and logistical support to ground troops. In addition, gaining control of Umm Qasr was essential to ensuring that Iraqi forces were denied access to the Persian Gulf. But equally important was the fact that gaining control of the port allowed coalition forces to begin humanitarian aid efforts, funneling tons of aid such as fresh water, dried food, medical supplies, and other items urgently needed by Iraqi citizens.

U.S. and British marines were able to overpower Iraqi forces and seize control of the port on March 21, 2003. Coalition mine-countermeasures forces were already working to clear the access waterways. Helicopters equipped with sophisticated sonar devices surveyed the waterways, helping to map the location of possible mines. Meanwhile, four U.S. minesweepers and six British minesweepers began a methodical trip up the Khor Abd Allah waterway leading to the Umm Qasr port. Using data fed from the helicopter surveys, the minesweepers carefully investigated each potential mine. Explosive charges were placed on mines and detonated. Almost simultaneously, U.S. naval forces intercepted a number of cleverly disguised Iraqi minelayers, preventing them from planting more than one hundred additional mines.

Once the marines had secured the port, navy sea, air, and land (SEAL) teams and other divers began work within the port waters. The teams used everything from high-tech unmanned underwater vehicles to trained dolphins to help hunt out mines.

Clearing the Waters of Iraq

One of the most serious challenges facing the U.S. Navy at the opening of Operation Iraqi Freedom was to clear mines laid by Iraqi forces so that coalition ships could utilize the port at Umm Qasr. A time-consuming and deadly important task, mine clearing was significantly aided in the war through the use of unusual technology.

In addition to the use of trained dolphins, the navy also utilized the REMUS autonomous underwater vehicle to aid in the task of making the port safe for coalition operations and an influx of humanitarian aid for Iraqi civilians.

The REMUS is a torpedo-shaped vehicle measuring less than three and a half feet long and weighing eighty pounds. Loaded with sensors and capable of operating at depths of up to one hundred meters, the REMUS uses side-scan sonar to detect minelike objects. Once an object is detected, it can be investigated by highly trained divers and explosive ordnance disposal divers.

In Iraq, the REMUS, dolphins, and human members of the mine sweeping naval team were able to clear the waters of mines in short order. The success opened the way for the port—Iraq's only deepwater port—to be used for ships to deliver humanitarian aid and coalition supplies.

Two explosives experts defuse mines taken from the waters around the Iraqi port of Umm Qasr.

Military officials lauded the use of the Marine Mammal System's bottlenose dolphins. The specially trained dolphins were airlifted to pools on nearby beaches, then dispatched to detect mines in shallow and silted waterways. Other dolphins were pooled in tanks aboard the USS *Gunston Hall* when not in action. With their built-in sensory sonar, the dolphins were able to identify potential mines in the murky water, and along with unmanned underwater vehicles, they helped streamline the process of identifying shapes as mines. For example, dolphins and unmanned vehicles were able to rule out debris such as car tires and oil drums, freeing human divers to deal with actual mines, which were destroyed by explosive ordnance specialists.

The mine detection and disposal forces cleared more than nine hundred nautical square miles of the Khor Abd Allah and Umm Qasr waterways. They identified 230 minelike objects, detected 90 mines, and destroyed those deemed a threat to shipping and naval operations. The navy regarded the enterprise as an unqualified success, noting that the operation was successful despite poor conditions ranging from minimal visibility to strong currents.

Special Operations

In addition to their minesweeping activities, navy SEALs performed other important duties during the opening hours of the Iraq War. Along with British Royal Marines, SEALs raided two gas and oil platforms in the Persian Gulf, capturing fifteen Iraqi soldiers and a large cache of weapons, including grenade launchers, AK-47 rifles, and surface-to-air missiles. Because 80 percent of Iraq's oil flowed through the platforms

The U.S. Navy used fast, heavily armored patrol boats like these to secure the harbors and coastlines of Iraq.

and into the holds of tankers, securing the platforms was considered essential. Had the Iraqi soldiers destroyed the facilities, Iraq would have lost a significant revenue stream. Moreover, environmental damage from the resulting spill could have been catastrophic. Some experts believed that oil in amounts equal to the environmentally devastating *Exxon Valdez* tanker spill in Alaska in 1989— some 11 million gallons—would have spilled into the Persian Gulf every two hours.

SEALs also surveyed and provided security on important waterways, patrolling in rigid-hull inflatable boats (RHIBs) and Mark V boats. RHIBs are utilized by special forces for intercept missions, such as stopping Iraqis from laying mines. Mark V boats, likewise used by special forces, are technically advanced high-speed craft designed to be transported quickly into a combat zone aboard an air force C-5 aircraft. The eighty-two-foot-long Mark V can insert or extract a team of sixteen navy SEALs, fully equipped, anywhere in the world within forty-eight hours.

To support operations, the SEALs used the *Joint Venture*, an aluminum-hulled catamaran modified to carry gunboats, amphibious landing craft, helicopters, and marine platoons, as an operational base near Umm Qasr. The *Joint Venture* provided supplies, shelter, and spare parts for the more than one dozen SEAL boats operating in the area.

Tomahawk Missiles

As important as such activities were to the overall war effort, however, the navy did not play a solely supportive role. Indeed, the navy contributed significant muscle to the war effort. Nowhere was that more apparent than in the navy's use of powerful Tomahawk missiles that struck with deadly force in the Iraq War.

Tomahawk missiles are what are known as cruise missiles, essentially pilotless flying bombs. A Tomahawk can be launched in any weather from either a surface ship or a submarine. The missiles are more than eighteen feet long and have a wingspan of more than nine feet. They can carry a conventional warhead weighing one thousand pounds. They can reach speeds of 550 miles per hour and have a range of 1,000 miles. As if its speed and range were not enough, however, the Tomahawk can fly at altitudes as low as one hundred feet, allowing it to elude detection by enemy radar.

The Tomahawk is a prime example of a standoff missile, essentially a weapon that can be fired from great distances and hit its targets with precision. The weapons are particularly valuable because they allow U.S. forces to deliver great firepower without jeopardizing the lives of the attacking sailors.

The Tomahawk is launched with a solid-fuel rocket engine and is later powered by a turbofan engine. A turbofan engine is equipped with a fan through which incoming air passes. The fan increases the thrust of the engine, making it more powerful while remaining fuel efficient. Equipped with contour-matching radar, the Tomahawk is guided to its target by matching internal digital maps to the terrain below. When the Tomahawk nears its target,

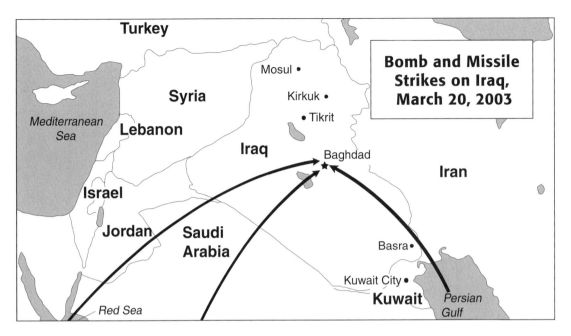

Bomb and Missile Strikes on Iraq, March 20, 2003

an optical system built into the weapon compares a stored image of the target with the actual target and guides the missile to its intended destination. Such precision is hardly cheap: Each Tomahawk missile costs about $1 million, and coalition forces used more than eight hundred of the missiles in the Iraq War. Nevertheless, so long as the missiles are programmed correctly, they are highly accurate and can hit enemy targets without unnecessarily jeopardizing innocent civilians.

Launching the Missiles

During the Iraq War, thirty-five coalition ships, a third of which were submarines, fired Tomahawk missiles between March 19 and April 3, 2003. Because of technological advances since the 1991 Gulf War, the lead time required between determining a tar-

get to launching a missile had been reduced dramatically. Whereas missions could take days to plan during previous conflicts, the time needed to program the Tomahawks had been reduced to a matter of hours. The result is that the missiles are now programmed with fresher intelligence, allowing the military to avoid what it euphemistically calls "unintended collateral damage." In other words, the missiles can hit their targets before targets have time to change positions and the missiles hit civilians instead.

On March 21, the night of the military's initial-stage bombardment campaign, thirty U.S. Navy and coalition ships launched more than 380 Tomahawk missiles against significant military targets. Ships ranging from the USS *Bunker Hill,* a cruiser that fired the first Tomahawk missile of Operation Iraqi Freedom, to the USS *John S. McCain,* an Aegis guided-missile destroyer, took part in the Tomahawk bombardment. In addition, two British ships, the HMS *Splendid* and the HMS *Turbulent*, also took part in the campaign.

A host of naval submarines also played significant roles in the Tomahawk bombardment. A record fifteen submarines participated in Operation Iraqi Freedom, including twelve U.S. subs. Two British subs and one Danish sub also participated. Nuclear-powered submarines from both the Atlantic and Pacific fleets streamed to the region to launch Tomahawk missiles during the conflict. Many of the U.S. subs that participated had already been at sea on other deployments when called to the Middle East. For example, the USS *Cheyenne*

had left Pearl Harbor in July 2002 for what sailors believed would be a six-month deployment. Instead, it was ordered to the Persian Gulf, where the *Cheyenne* became the first sub to launch a Tomahawk missile in a deployment that ended up lasting nine months. "At the time, we had no idea we'd be the first submarine to launch a Tomahawk," said Commander Charles Doty, the *Cheyenne*'s commanding officer. "We just knew we had to execute our mission, and the crew reacted magnificently. There were a lot of U.S. forces involved, and I'm glad to know USS *Cheyenne* was able to support

A Tomahawk missile launches toward an Iraqi target. Coalition forces used such guided missiles to destroy distant military targets.

the coalition effort in Iraq and help liberate the Iraqi people."[5]

Submarines were not the only naval ships that endured long tours of duty. In December 2002 the fifty-five hundred officers and sailors of the USS *Abraham Lincoln* had been headed to San Diego after six months of supporting the war effort in Afghanistan. But the crew then received orders to turn around and prepare for war in Iraq. During the next four months, the aircraft carrier handled more than fifteen hundred combat sorties, or individual missions. By the time the ship's duty tour in Iraq had been completed, the *Abraham Lincoln* had been deployed 290 consecutive days and had traveled more than one hundred thousand miles.

Medical Support

Although much of the navy's effort was necessarily aimed at destroying the Iraqi regime of Saddam Hussein, the U.S. Navy also provided much-needed medical care. In mid-March 2003 the USNS *Comfort* arrived in the region to provide hospital-quality medical care to both military and civilian casualties. The ship's doctors and nurses treated injured coalition forces, Iraqi freedom fighters, Iraqi citizens, and Iraqi prisoners of war (POWs). Strictly following the protocols of the Geneva Convention, an internationally agreed upon set of rules for the treatment of prisoners of war, the *Comfort* treated patients on the basis of medical need, not based on which side they were fighting.

The first combat casualties treated aboard the *Comfort* began to arrive on March 20. By the time the ship had departed in May 2003, its medical staff had provided trauma care to more than 196 Iraqi POWs and civilians. In all, the *Comfort*'s crew provided extensive service during the Iraq War.

The Submarine's Role in Operation Iraqi Freedom

Although Iraq is mostly a landlocked country and Saddam Hussein lacked a significant navy, U.S. Navy submarines were key participants in combat operations that ultimately led to the successful overthrow of the Iraqi dictator.

During Operation Iraqi Freedom, twelve U.S. submarines and two British submarines conducted the largest-ever submarine-launched Tomahawk missile strike. Submarine commanders and their crews were lauded for their efforts in the war, with some receiving special recognition.

Commander William J. Frake, commanding officer of the USS *Montpelier*, for example, was awarded the Bronze Star upon his return home.

In a navy press release announcing the honor, dated December 3, 2003, and headlined "Three Sub Commanders Awarded Bronze Star for OIF," Frake said, "For me personally, it's more of an honor for my crew. After all the shooting was done, and the crew was coming up and congratulating me, I told them that they were the ones who did everything. I just said 'shoot.'"

According to the release, found at the U.S. Navy Web site, the Bronze Star was established by President Franklin D. Roosevelt in 1944 to reward those who distinguish themselves in military combat operations through either heroism or meritorious achievement.

To put the ship's record in perspective, the doctors of the *Comfort* performed 337 surgical procedures during the 1991 Gulf War. During the first five weeks of Operation Iraqi Freedom, by contrast, the *Comfort*'s doctors had performed more than 590 surgeries. In addition, more than 2,400 X-ray studies were performed, and 600 units of blood were transfused in support of the *Comfort*'s fifty-bed trauma area and twelve-room surgical complex.

The navy also provided medical services on land. For the first time, the navy utilized what it called an expeditionary medical facility, essentially a prepackaged field hospital that had been prepositioned in the region, shipped to Iraq, and set up near combat zones to treat injured soldiers

The USNS Comfort *has twelve operating rooms, a medical laboratory, pharmacy, and beds for one thousand patients.*

and civilians. Overall, the expeditionary medical facility treated some eleven hundred patients, roughly half of whom were Iraqis. Casualties needing additional medical attention were sent to the *Comfort* at sea.

The hospital was staffed by the legendary "Devil Docs," naval doctors whose primary job is to treat injured U.S. Marine Corps personnel. However, the Devil Docs treated anyone who came through their doors in their sophisticated, mobile emergency room facilities. One member of the Devil Doc team noted that when a patient arrived, it did not matter whether he or she was an American or an Iraqi. "They're all human beings who have souls. They all have pain. They all bleed the same, so we must save them all,"[6] said Petty Officer Second Class Sonya M. Hamrick, a pharmacy technician. Added navy lieutenant Kevin R. Poole, a physician's assistant, "If you don't do that, you're playing God."[7]

The facilities operated twenty-four hours a day, so the medical crew worked long hours. At the height of the war, more than one patient an hour was being treated in the shock, stabilization, and triage unit. Despite the long hours, most of the medical team expressed satisfaction in their work. Said Lieutenant Thomas A. Olson, a physician's assistant, "I get by on drinking a lot of coffee and drive. You learn that there are certain situations that you can't worry about sleep. You must focus and get the job done first. I'm glad we have the chance to do this job."[8]

The injured could likewise be thankful for the work of the Devil Docs. In previous wars, those who died of wounds after reaching medical care ranged between 10 and 15 percent. During Operation Iraqi Freedom, however, the figure was cut to 3 percent. "In Operation Iraqi Freedom, if a wounded Soldier or Marine made it to our medical units, they all survived. That's a tremendous accomplishment,"[9] said Captain John Sentell, commanding officer of the naval hospital facility in Jacksonville, Florida, which deployed personnel to the Iraq War.

The navy's presence in the Iraq War helped to hasten the end of the conflict. The navy provided devastating firepower through Tomahawk missiles launched by both surface ships and submarines. And because war inevitably brings casualties, the navy's medical care facilities brought top-notch care to injured soldiers. However, the major attack on the Iraqi military came from the air.

☆ Chapter 2 ☆

Aircraft over Iraq: The Fixed-Wing Arsenal

As in the Gulf War, U.S. airpower was a significant factor in the Iraq War. Along with the Tomahawk missiles fired from naval vessels, U.S. aircraft launched what the military called a shock-and-awe campaign against Iraq designed to destroy the enemy's willingness to fight and to knock out the leadership and infrastructure the Iraqi military needed to resist the onslaught. Enjoying nearly unfettered air superiority and utilizing the world's most sophisticated aircraft, U.S. and coalition planes were able to crisscross Iraq with impunity, delivering high-tech weaponry with deadly accuracy.

The Air Force Role

The coalition relied on swarms of the most technologically advanced fighting planes and bombers ever assembled for warfare. Utilizing aircraft ranging from Vietnam War–era B-52 bombers to the latest in stealth aircraft, the coalition forces enjoyed unbridled control of the skies over Iraq.

The U.S. Air Force dominated the coalition's airpower. During the first thirty days of Operation Iraqi Freedom, the air force flew more than twenty-four thousand sorties—nearly 60 percent of the coalition total. Of those, roughly ninety-three hundred were combat related. These missions were carried out by a variety of planes, which each had specialized, complementary functions.

The B-52 Stratofortress

The air force's B-52 Stratofortress—a plane that has been the U.S. workhorse of manned strategic bombers for more than forty years—again proved its reliability and dependability during the Iraq War. Originally intended to carry and deliver nuclear weapons, the B-52 is capable of launching the widest array of weapons of any bomber in the U.S. fleet. Among its payloads are so-called dumb bombs, which are simply dropped and explode on impact; and their high-technology counterparts, 2,000-pound

The B-52 Stratofortress was used to deliver bomb loads during the opening phases of the war against Iraq.

precision-guided "smart bombs." The huge planes have a wingspan of 185 feet and can fly at speeds of up to 650 miles per hour at heights of up to 50,000 feet. The planes weigh 185,000 pounds unloaded, but they become airborne with the help of their eight engines, which each provide 17,000 pounds of thrust. Carrying a crew of five, the B-52 is outfitted with sophisticated electro-optical viewing systems to aid in targeting, assessing battles, and improving safety. The B-52 has enormous range: It is able to fly an astounding 8,800 miles without refueling.

The B-52 played a large role in the opening air salvo of Operation Iraqi Freedom. The enormous planes dropped tons of precision-guided weapons on key Iraqi command and control targets to devastating effect. After scrambling to ready the planes for their missions, many support personnel gathered in front of televisions to watch the planes they prepared deliver their payloads of bombs over Iraq. "To see the results was unbelievable. You're working hard and training every day to achieve the kind of success we had today. It was an unbelievable feeling,"[10] said Staff Sergeant Randy Simmons, a crew chief.

Stealth Aircraft

In sharp contrast to the B-52 is the B-2 Spirit, a stealth bomber that provides the service with flexibility and a high degree of effectiveness. The plane is designed to penetrate the most sophisticated defense systems in the world and to attack an enemy's most heavily defended targets. The Spirit is difficult for enemy forces to see and track, a characteristic that is further enhanced by the B-2's ability to operate at high altitudes—up to fifty thousand feet. High-altitude operations, in turn, increase the plane's range and provide its crew of two with better visibility.

Although much of the technology that makes the B-2 a stealth craft remains classified, it is known that the plane gives off reduced infrared, acoustic, electromagnetic, visual, and radar "signatures," the signals that identify an object's size, shape, location, and speed. Consequently, enemy tracking systems yield confused, inaccurate readings. Composite materials, special coatings, and the plane's distinctive low-profile "flying wing" design make it difficult for enemy forces to see and pursue.

The planes have a wingspan of 172 feet, can carry a payload of forty thousand pounds, and can fly six thousand nautical miles without being refueled. According to an air force assessment, the aircraft's large range and payload capacity make the B-2 a highly efficient bomber. The air force says that two B-2s armed with precision-guided bombs can do the work of seventy-five conventional bombers. During Operation Iraqi Freedom, B-2s flew missions from as far away as Whiteman Air Force Base in Missouri and from the island of Diego Garcia in the Indian Ocean to participate in the coalition air campaign.

Strike Eagles

Although less exotic than the B-2, the F-15E Strike Eagle also provides tremendous firepower and flexibility to air force attacks. The plane is designed both to fight enemy planes in the sky and to launch missiles against targets on land. The Strike Eagle's two-person crew comprises a pilot and a weapons-systems officer. The aircraft is

The B-2 bomber employed stealth technology to evade enemy radar during missions deep inside Iraq.

Coalition Strategy

The clear superiority of the United States and coalition in the skies over Iraq allowed for a rapid ground offensive in the opening moments of Operation Iraqi Freedom. Moreover, that air superiority allowed the coalition to provide close air support to those ground troops that found themselves boxed in by the Iraqi military.

In an often repeated ritual, hundreds of coalition bombers, helicopters, and slow-moving but highly effective A-10 Warthog planes hammered Iraqi troops well before coalition ground forces even met them. And once ground troops did make contact with enemy forces, those same planes were there to rain precision weapons on the Iraqis to make the going easier for coalition ground forces.

According to Sonya Ross and Chris Tomlinson of the Associated Press, airpower was a constant threat to the Iraqis. Ross and Tomlinson quote Michele Flournoy, a defense policy expert at the Center for Strategic and International Studies, as saying that the use of air assets provided ground troops with an extra attacker in close quarters: "If a particular unit gets overmatched, gets isolated, close air support can come in, rebalance the playing field, provide the additional firepower and get those forces out of trouble."

The slow-moving A-10 Warthog was vital in destroying Iraqi troop concentrations and tank units from the air.

engineered to fight enemy planes en route to a target, strike the target, and then fight its way back to base. The plane is also fast, reaching speeds in excess of Mach 2.5—nearly nineteen hundred miles an hour—with a range of twenty-four hundred miles without refueling.

The Strike Eagle's sophisticated navigation system relies on a laser gyroscope that continuously monitors the plane's position and feeds real-time information to the plane's central computer and operating systems, including the digital maps in the plane's two cockpits—one for the pilot and one for the aircraft's weapons-systems officer. The plane's radar system, meantime, allows crews to detect ground targets from long range. The system simultaneously allows the pilot to search the area for enemy planes.

During the Iraq War, Strike Eagles performed a variety of tasks. In addition to flying hundreds of bombing missions, Strike Eagles also provided close air support for ground forces, bombing enemy forces that threatened coalition soldiers. This versatility made the plane an integral part of the coalition attack. Although the air force is developing a new fighter-bomber to replace the Strike Eagle, military analysts believe the F-15E will continue to be a major air asset in the U.S. force through 2020.

The air force used the F-15E Strike Eagle to patrol the skies.

Strike Eagles are outfitted with the low-altitude navigation and targeting infrared for night (LANTIRN) system, which allows them to be flown at low altitudes day or night and even in poor weather to attack enemy targets. The system is a major factor in the Strike Eagle's reputation as one of the most accurate bombers in the world. One former air force commander noted that two F-15Es loaded with twelve thousand pounds of conventional bombs can destroy a target with the same effectiveness as eight of the aircraft's predecessors carrying forty-eight thousand pounds of bombs.

Navy and Marine Planes

The air force, of course, was not the only branch of the service with valuable airborne assets in the war. With its five carriers in the region, the U.S. Navy and U.S. Marine Corps also contributed valuable firepower from the air. More than 780 navy and marine aircraft joined the fight, flying almost fourteen thousand sorties during the military phase of the war—an average of fifteen hundred sorties per day. Navy pilots flew nearly nine thousand missions, more than fifty-five hundred of which were combat sorties. The remainder were refueling, command-and-control, and support sorties.

Navy pilots remained on the offensive even after President Bush declared the war effectively over on May 1, 2003. On November 28, 2003, for example, a navy F/A-18 Hornet from the carrier USS *Enterprise* in the northern Persian Gulf attacked Iraqi troops who were directing mortar fire at coalition forces near Baqubah, Iraq. The Hornet dropped a single one-thousand-pound bomb, putting an end to the skirmish.

The Hornet is the workhorse carrier-based combat plane. It contains a multinode radar that is equally effective in air-to-air and air-to-ground missions. The plane is outfitted with an advanced array of avionics, cockpit displays, and weaponry, and its aerodynamics allow pilots tremendous maneuverability. Powered by two General Electric F404-400 afterburning turbofans, which provide 32,000 pounds of thrust, the Hornet can reach speeds of 1,190 miles per hour and climb 45,000 feet per minute. During Operation Iraqi Freedom, Hornets dropped 380,000 pounds of bombs on Iraqi troops and installations.

AC-130H/U Gunships

As powerful and effective as the military's fighters and bombers are, however, they were not designed to absorb enemy fire while at the same time providing close air support to ground troops or to perform armed reconnaisance missions. The military has a number of other types of planes that perform these and other functions. For example, the AC-130H/U gunship helped to provide armed reconnaissance— essentially low-altitude aerial patrols—and provided direct support to ground troops engaged with Iraqi soldiers.

The AC-130H/U is a heavily armed aircraft that features side-firing weapons. Outfitted with sophisticated sensor, navigation, and fire-control systems, the gunship is able to provide accurate fire in support of coalition ground troops. Moreover, high-tech sensors allow gunship operators to identify friendly ground forces under any conditions, minimizing the risks of so-called friendly fire—shooting at one's own soldiers. The plane is capable of operating in any light or weather condition, making it an extremely flexible and valuable part of the military's arsenal of planes.

The gunship is relatively slow, achieving a maximum speed of only three hundred miles per hour. But it bristles with deadly weaponry, including both a 40-millimeter cannon and a 105-millimeter cannon. The AC-130H/U carries a thirteen-man crew: a pilot, copilot, navigator, fire-control officer, electronic warfare officer, flight engineer, TV operator, infrared de-

The AH-130H Spectre provided support to ground troops.

tection set operator, loadmaster, and four aerial gunners.

The Warthog

Another deadly plane designed to provide close air support for ground troops is the A-10/OA-10 Thunderbolt II, perhaps better known by its nickname, the Warthog. The first air force plane designed especially to provide support and cover for ground forces, the Warthog is heavily armored. Titanium armor protects the plane's pilots and flight-control system, and built-in redundancies in the plane's structural design further enhance the ability of the craft to take heavy fire and yet return safely to base. The plane is built to withstand direct hits from armor-piercing and high-explosive projectiles up to twenty-three millimeters. Manual systems allow pilots to fly and land when hydraulic power is lost.

The plane got its nickname because it is slow and unattractive. But that does not mean it is unappreciated. The Warthog is equipped with thirty-millimeter GAU-8/A Gatling guns, which can fire nearly four thousand rounds a minute and are capable of taking out enemy tanks and other armored vehicles. Night-vision goggles enable pilots to operate the Warthog in darkness. These weapons systems make the Warthog indispensable in aiding ground troops pinned down by enemy forces.

The plane was designed for easy maintenance. The Warthog can be serviced and operated from bases with limited facilities near battlefields, and many of the aircraft's parts are interchangeable for speed and ease of repair.

Warthogs rescued many soldiers from potentially deadly situations during Operation Iraqi Freedom. In one incident, a pilot nicknamed "Donut" was flying support for a convoy of special operations forces who encountered Iraqi resistance. Donut's cover fire allowed the troops to effect a temporary retreat and a rendezvous with other U.S. soldiers. The ability to give tangible aid to troops on the ground proved the most satisfying aspect of a Warthog pilot's job. "I quantify it by the guy on the radio saying, 'Thanks, you saved our bacon,'"[11] said Donut.

Frequency Management

Thousands of coalition planes flew over Iraq during the war, conducting myriad missions ranging from reconnaissance to support to bombing. As difficult as it was to keep all the planes on mission and out of each other's way, military officials faced a perhaps even more daunting challenge—managing the more than five thousand electronic frequencies used for communications to make all those flights a reality.

It was a huge challenge, but the Combined Forces Air Component Command (CFACC) had to meet it or risk the lives of pilots and the success of missions. In a special report on the CFACC by Bob Jensen, "Theater Frequency Management Organizes Airwaves," Master Sergeant John C. Zimmermann, the CFACC's theater-frequency manager, discusses the process of frequency management:

Frequency management is a process to ensure all equipment emitting radio frequency energy work harmoniously within the electromagnetic battlespace. That battlespace includes basically everything that supports the fighting mission. For instance, each of the satellites we use has their own frequencies. Each of the various radars operate in different bands and within those bands they're assigned their own frequencies. Every aircraft also has its own frequencies to work with their specific radios. So to give you an example . . . I'm trying to make sure the satellite we're using to control (an unmanned aerial vehicle) with isn't going to interfere with the (Navy fighter pilot) the (airborne warning and control system) crews are talking to.

Just as the air campaign itself required careful choreography, so did the process of managing radio frequencies.

Support Aircraft

Keeping all the coalition aircraft in the air to complete their missions was a monumental task that required delicate choreography as well as the ability to refuel the planes in flight. Responsibility for making sure the coalition's aircraft were able to operate safely and remain adequately fueled fell to specialized support aircraft, which played a critical role in the ability of the military to conduct extensive air campaigns that helped destroy the enemy's command-and-control structure, provide support to ground troops, and hasten the end of the conflict.

Among the most important planes in keeping the air attack from becoming a disaster was the E-3 Sentry, better known as the airborne warning and control system (AWACS). With the ability to operate under any weather condition, the plane provided surveillance, command-and-control, and communications functions that were essential in ensuring that coalition aircraft reached their intended targets without hitting each other. The plane, essentially a retrofitted commercial Boeing 707, is distinguished by its rotating radar dome attached to the top of the plane's fuselage. The radar is highly powerful and sophisticated, with a range of more than 250 miles for low-flying targets. It is equipped with special equipment that allows operators to distinguish between enemy and friendly planes. The AWACS performs many functions, ranging from surveillance to serving as a flying air traffic control tower.

The AWACS is built to be jam resistant, and it proved its mettle when successfully performing missions even when bombarded with heavy electronic-jamming signals by enemy forces. Air force officials believe the AWACS presents a distinct advantage to ground-based radar systems because, unlike a fixed radar station on land, the plane's flight path can be quickly changed if necessary to elude enemy attack. The radar system's long range also allows the AWACS to operate out of harm's way. Without refueling, an AWACS can stay aloft for eight hours; with refueling, it could theoretically stay in the air indefinitely. Equipped with an onboard crew rest area, crews can work in shifts for round-the-clock operations.

During Operation Iraqi Freedom, the AWACS helped choreograph the extensive coalition air campaign and was instrumental in helping the military take advantage of so-called targets of opportunity—Iraqi troops or equipment that unexpectedly came into view. For example, when ground troops were fighting to seize control of an airfield, an AWACS directed an F-16 to the scene to eliminate enemy vehicles. Although the first priority of an AWACS crew was to aid successful coalition attacks, they were mindful of the human cost of their operations. "The first time we crossed over into Iraqi airspace, it was different seeing the little green plots of earth the Iraqi people had been preparing for spring planting," said Major Chuck Diven, mission crew commander of the 970th Airborne Air Control Squadron. "I

thought, 'that could be my yard.' It totally changed my perspective on things."[12]

Refueling Planes

A successful air campaign would have been nearly impossible if not for specially designed in-flight refueling planes. Aerial refueling allowed coalition craft to be in the air twenty-four hours a day, likewise forcing Iraqi forces to be on alert at all times. Colonel Cathy Clothier, commander of the 401st Air Expeditionary Operations Group, realized the importance of her group's mission as it prepared for its first refueling mission over Iraq. She said, "I briefed all our aircrew about the upcoming operations and told them what we were about to do in the next few days would change history. Not a single bomb gets dropped, not a single air-to-air engagement happens, or missile is fired unless tankers make it happen. I'm proud of our people here."[13]

One workhorse of the refueling fleet is the KC-135 Stratotanker. The Stratotanker is powered by four turbofans that allow the plane to get airborne with takeoff weights of more than 161,000 tons. The plane is capable of delivering up to 100,000 tons of fuel. An operator located at the rear of the plane controls a flying boom that delivers fuel to aircraft ranging from bombers to fighter jets from U.S. and allied armed forces. The Stratotanker also is configured with a cargo deck above the refueling system, which can hold both passengers and cargo. A contingent of 149 Stratotankers helped keep the coalition adequately fueled during Operation Iraqi Freedom.

The Stratotanker has been supplemented by the KC-10 Extender, an advanced craft designed to provide increased flexibility to the U.S. armed forces. The Extender combines the role of tanker and cargo aircraft, with the ability to carry fighter support personnel and equipment on overseas deployments. It can carry up to seventy-five people and almost 170,000 pounds of cargo up to forty-four hundred miles without refueling, all while carrying more than 356,000 pounds of fuel in its three large fuel tanks. Fuel can be transferred to another plane at a rate of up to eleven hundred gallons per minute. Making the plane even more versatile, it can itself be refueled, either by a Stratotanker or another Extender. Thirty-three Extenders were active in the Iraq War.

The contributions of the tankers were enormous to the coalition war effort. Over the first thirty days of Operation Iraqi Freedom, air force tankers delivered 376 million pounds of jet fuel, 90 percent of the total amount of fuel delivered in the sky.

Cargo Craft

The United States used its airpower in other ways, including delivering ground

A KC-135 Stratotanker refueling plane leads a formation of coalition fighter aircraft over Iraq.

"Everything . . . Is Logistics"

The coalition air campaign appeared to be seamless, with constant missions being flown all over Iraq with no letup for Iraqi soldiers. Through the use of high-tech planes and precision weaponry, the coalition was able to fly anywhere and bomb whatever target necessary to accomplish the war's aims of defeating the Iraqi military and driving Saddam Hussein from power.

While the pilots of these planes drew most of the credit, a great deal of the success of the war can be attributed to command and support troops on the ground. Troops like U.S. Marine Corps major Jonathan Pirkey, a watch officer for the Marine Liaison Office in the Combined Air Operations Center, helped make decisions that allowed the air war to be conducted successfully.

Pirkey says a successful air campaign was a simple matter of logistics. Navy chief petty officer Douglas Stutz quotes Pirkey in a U.S. Air Force Web site article, "Logistical Thinking from the Ground to Air":

Everything in the world is logistics. Everyone might laugh, but it's true if you think about it. Putting fuel in a plane is a form of supply and demand. Flying that aircraft on a mission is taking the air asset from point A to point B to accomplish a specific task. Even targeting a site with precision-guided munitions is just a different way of delivering supplies. Those of us who are experts in logistics might not pull triggers and actually win battles in combat, but we ensure our side can wage war quicker, safer and better than the other side. That's what we do, and we do it very well.

The story said Pirkey was well aware that his efforts were important in the Iraq War. "Even though I'm not a pilot, to be able to help direct the allied effort to remove Saddam Hussein's regime from Iraq is a very cool thing," Pirkey said.

soldiers and their heavy machinery to the battlefield. For example, in one major operation conducted at night, fifteen C-17s air-dropped one thousand army paratroopers and forty vehicles into northern Iraq. The C-17 is the newest and most flexible cargo craft in the air force arsenal. It is capable of rapidly delivering troops and their equipment into any war area. Cargo is loaded through a large aft door that accommodates military vehicles and large pallets of supplies. Though an enormous plane, it is operated by a crew of just three—pilot, copilot, and loadmaster. The C-17 is 174 feet long and has a wingspan of 169 feet, 10 inches. The plane is powered by four F117-PW-100 engines, each of which has 40,440 pounds of thrust.

The fixed-wing airpower brought to bear by coalition forces was possibly the most technologically sophisticated assembly of aircraft ever gathered for war. With a combination of quickness, stealth, and sheer toughness, coalition aircraft were a formidable opponent for the Iraqis. Nevertheless, the fixed-wing bombers, fighter jets, and support aircraft told only half the story of coalition airpower. Helicopters also figured prominently in the story of the air war over Iraq.

Chapter 3

Helicopters in Iraq: "If They Move, We'll Go After Them"

The tremendous airpower of the United States delivered a devastating blow to Iraqi forces and that nation's command-and-control system, significantly easing the way for the coalition ground offensive. However, fixed-wing craft were far from the only planes to contribute to the war effort. Helicopters provided an essential element of the U.S.-led attack, providing close air support to ground troops, evacuating trapped or injured soldiers, and delivering troops into battle.

Helicopters first gained wide use in warfare during the Vietnam War. In that conflict, the UH-1 helicopter, better known as the Huey, first proved its essential utility by carrying supplies, transporting troops, and evacuating soldiers from the battlefield in jungle or mountain conditions where airfields were limited. The Huey was equipped with machine guns, but pilots saw room for improvement. They rigged up crude rocket tubes on the Huey, and through battlefield ingenuity, they created the world's first attack helicopters.

The military—and manufacturers—seized on the innovation. Bell Helicopter developed the Cobra attack helicopter in 1966, and by 1970 it had delivered some one thousand Cobras to the army.

The AH-1W Super Cobra

Helicopters have played a role in all U.S. military operations since Vietnam, prominently in the Iraq War. A Cobra significantly modified since the Vietnam era is a prime example. The AH-1W Super Cobra attack helicopter, which is used by the U.S. Marine Corps, saw widespread duty in Iraq. Its primary mission is to provide close air support for troops, to take out tanks and other helicopters, and to provide armed escort for choppers carrying troops.

The Cobra is equipped with devastatingly deadly weaponry. It carries a twenty-millimeter minigun capable of firing 750 rounds, forty-millimeter grenade launchers, and an array of rocket pods carrying air-to-surface missiles. The Cobra is outfitted with laser and infrared targeting systems designed to launch missiles effectively used against other helicopters and tanks or in defense of troops on the ground. The Cobra can operate day or night and in adverse weather conditions. As part of its self-defense package, the Cobra is equipped with chaff and flare dispensers. These decoys can be ejected when heat-seeking weapons are zeroing in on the craft, confusing the weapons and allowing the Cobra to escape unscathed.

The Cobra is 58 feet long and stands nearly 14 feet tall. The two-seat, twin-engine Cobra is capable of both land and sea operations and can travel at speeds of up to 169 miles per hour. The copter has a maximum takeoff weight of 14,750 pounds and has a range of nearly 300 miles. The Cobra can be operated at altitudes of up to 18,700 feet.

During the 1991 Gulf War, Cobras destroyed ninety-seven tanks, more than one hundred armored personnel carriers and vehicles, sixteen bunkers, and two antiaircraft batteries without suffering a single loss. The Cobra similarly served with distinction in the Iraq War. When, early in the conflict, some U.S. troops were trapped in heavy fighting in Nasiriyah, Cobra helicopters joined in with Warthog airplanes and F/A-18 Hornets to stifle Iraqi forces. Cobras helped to destroy ten Iraqi tanks, an artillery battery, and an antiaircraft gun. Later in the war, Cobra helicopters helped tip the bal-

Helicopter Basics

Seeing a helicopter on the ground, many people wonder how such a craft can fly. Its long, slender blades appear inadequate to lift and power the helicopter into flight.

However, each of a helicopter's blades on the main rotor is like a miniature airplane wing, and as they spin, these blades provide lift that helps the craft get airborne. By adjusting the pitch, or tilt, of these blades, a helicopter pilot can easily maneuver the craft. By increasing the pitch of all the blades equally, the pilot can take the copter straight up. By changing the pitch unequally, the pilot can steer the helicopter in a given direction.

The rotating blades of the main rotor exert a spinning force on the entire craft. Without a stabilizing mechanism, a helicopter would spin in circles. To stabilize a helicopter, tail rotor blades spin sideways, countering the rotation created by the main rotor blades.

ance in favor of marines who had been caught in a battle with an elite Iraqi Republican Guard unit forty-five miles south of Baghdad in a city called Aziziya. Joining B-52s and F/A-18 Hornets, Cobra helicopters helped silence Iraqi opposition. Many Iraqi forces attempted to flee, but commanders were unsympathetic. Major Matt Feringa, who was responsible for coordinating air support for the advancing marine unit, said the Iraqi troops would be shown no mercy. "I wouldn't want to be in their shoes right now. They are being bombed all the time. If they move, we'll go after them. If they just stay there, we'll find them."[14]

The Apache

Newer, faster, and more advanced than the Cobra, the Apache AH-64 attack helicopter is possibly the most feared helicopter in the world. Sometimes described as a "fly-ing tank," the Apache helicopter is designed to survive heavy attack and still inflict massive damage to enemy forces. Indeed, the Apache can fly for thirty minutes after losing its oil, enough time to finish its

The Cobra

The Cobra helicopter is a direct descendant of the UH-1 Huey helicopter developed for the U.S. Army during the Vietnam War. After troops modified the Huey to become an attack helicopter, engineers went to work to develop a helicopter specifically designed to be used as an offensive attack craft.

The result was the Cobra, which is sleeker and more heavily armed than the Huey. Modified ex-tensively since first introduced in the 1960s, today's Cobra is one of the most feared helicopters in military use. The highly versatile craft is utilized in a variety of roles, ranging from armed escort of ground forces to attacking enemy forces that are threatening ground troops.

The heavily armed AH-1W Super Cobra helicopter was designed to serve as an offensive attack craft.

An Apache helicopter launches flares to distract incoming heat-seeking missiles.

mission and fly to safety. The Apache has two engines and a top speed of 192 miles per hour. It is operated by a crew of two: The pilot sits in the rear of the cockpit, while the copilot/gunner, or weapons operator, sits in the front seat.

The Apache is usually tasked to take out armored targets on the ground, such as tanks or enemy bunkers. To help accomplish its task, the Apache is outfitted with up to sixteen powerful Hellfire missiles. The Apache also can be outfitted with rocket launchers, whose payload in Iraq included folding-fin 2.75-inch aerial rockets. Apache gunners can fire the rockets individually or in groups. A host of sophisticated aids help weapons operators to aim, including a target acquisition designation sight that combines highly accurate optical sensors and laser range finders. Another innovation is the pilot's night-vision sensor, which is linked to infrared sensors on the front of the Apache. Those sensors project images onto a monocle lens in front of the pilot's right eye, allowing a clear view of the battlefield in all weather and light conditions. The sensors follow the turn of the pilot's head, automatically adjusting the view of the battlefield in all directions.

The Apache also is equipped with an M230 thirty-millimeter automatic cannon, which is attached to a turret under the Apache's nose. Aided by a highly sophisticated computer system, the gunner is able to maneuver the turret in nearly every direction. The Apache also has an automatic cannon, which utilizes what is known as a chain-gun design. An electric motor rotates the chain, which in turn slides the bolt assembly back and forth to load, fire, extract, and eject cartridges. This gun can fire up to 650 rounds a minute.

High-Technology Features of Apaches

The Apache helicopter has a radar dome attached to its mast. The radar system allows crew members to detect ground forces, aircraft, and buildings. A sophisticated signal processor compares the shapes to a stored database of potential targets, and the Apache's onboard computer automatically pinpoints the targets on the gunner's display panel.

Other features of the Apache help pilots to elude enemy fire. For example, if enemy radar is detected, pilots can activate a radar jammer to prevent enemy forces from pinpointing the helicopter's exact location. Moreover, the Apache is designed to be operated at low altitudes, a posture that helps it to hide behind terrain before attacking. The Apache's sophisticated engineering also helps it evade heat-seeking missiles, primarily through what is known as the Black Hole infrared suppression system. This system reduces the amount of heat energy that emanates from the helicopter—the Apache's infrared signature—by mixing hot engine exhaust with cooler air flowing around the helicopter and passing it through a special filter. The Apache also is outfitted with an infrared jammer, a device that releases varying amounts of infrared radiation. This jamming system makes it difficult for enemy forces to accurately lock in heat-seeking missiles on Apache helicopters.

As the military's primary attack helicopter, the Apache is protected by special armor when it is unable to avoid direct enemy fire. Portions of the copter are clad with relatively lightweight, soft Kevlar, the same material used in bulletproof vests. The Apache's cockpit is protected by reinforced armor as well as bulletproof glass. The Apache is designed to withstand attacks from 12.7-millimeter ammunition, and key engine and helicopter rotor parts can take hits from 23-millimeter ammunition and not be seriously compromised.

The Apache played a significant role in the Iraq War. For example, on March 23, 2003, a group of thirty-two Apaches attacked elite Iraqi Republican Guard units in a fierce firefight that lasted some three hours. The Apaches attacked the Second Armored Brigade of the Medina Division of the Republican Guard, a unit made up of troops considered most loyal to Saddam Hussein. Destroying the Republican Guard division was considered essential because the division had been blocking an important approach to Baghdad. After a softening air campaign designed to knock out the unit's radar and antiaircraft artillery, the Apaches took off from Najaf, south of Baghdad, and were successful in knocking out a number of Iraqi T-72 battle tanks, the most advanced enemy tank.

Apaches were not always on the giving end of intense fire in the March 23 battle, however. The Republican Guards had been warned of the attack by an Iraqi observer in Najaf, and they returned intense fire despite the softening-up air strikes. Colonel Daniel Ball, who commanded the Apache unit, said, "Every single one of the Apaches that went out on the mission took between ten and twenty hits from antiaircraft fire, rocket-propelled grenades and surface-to-air missiles."[15] After the battle commanders decided that the helicopters were better suited to a supporting role. The Apaches were then used almost exclusively for armed reconaissance

The primary mission of Black Hawk helicopters was to transport troops to the battlefield and evacuate the injured.

and close air support, not as a major offensive spearhead for ground forces.

Black Hawk Helicopters

Not all helicopters in the U.S. fleet are designed for offensive combat. Many, like the Huey, are designed primarily for use as transport helicopters. Perhaps the most well-known transport helicopter, or utility helicopter, in the military fleet is the army's UH-60 Black Hawk, which can travel at speeds of up to 184 miles per hour. The helicopter uses two turboshaft engines to power its fifty-four-foot main rotor, and an eleven-foot tail rotor helps provide extra lift. The Black Hawk is operated by crews of three or four and is designed to carry an entire eleven-man infantry squad. The Black Hawk can deploy a 105-millimeter

howitzer and thirty rounds of ammunition. The Black Hawk also can be utilized as an aeromedical evacuation vehicle, transporting wounded soldiers.

The Black Hawk is armored to allow it to get soldiers to battlefields or to swoop in and retrieve trapped soldiers. The pilot and copilot sit in armor-protected seats, and protective armor on the helicopter itself can withstand direct hits from twenty-three-millimeter shells. Machine guns can be mounted on the doors of the Black Hawk, and the copter is equipped with systems to help it elude heat-seeking munitions. For example, the Black Hawk can disperse chaff and infrared jamming flares.

Because they routinely fly under very hazardous conditions, Black Hawks have a high risk of being shot down. On November 15, 2003, for example, twelve coalition troops died and nine were injured when two Black Hawks collided over Mosul, Iraq. Eyewitnesses said the helicopters crashed when a missile was fired and one of the copters attempted to dodge the missile. The Black Hawks had been attempting to aid an ambushed U.S. foot patrol. However, given the fact that Black Hawk helicopters flew hundreds of missions during Operation Iraqi Freedom, relatively few were shot from the sky, with fewer than ten reported incidents.

The versatile Black Hawk has been modified for use in other branches of the U.S. armed services. For example, the air force utilizes what it calls the HH-60 Pave Hawk, which it uses for search-and-rescue missions, medical evacuations, and disaster relief. The navy, by contrast, utilizes its SH-60 Sea Hawk for such missions as antisubmarine and antiship warfare, special forces operations, and cargo transport.

The Chinook

Another important army helicopter is the CH-47 Chinook, which was utilized extensively during Operation Iraqi Freedom. The twin-engine, heavy-lift cargo helicopter is operated by a four-person crew that includes two pilots, one flight engineer, and one crew chief. It is capable of delivering up to forty-four combat troops to battle or heavy cargo and supplies. The Chinook can carry a 19,500-pound load, which is almost twice the load-carrying capacity of the original Chinooks developed for use in the Vietnam War. A triple-hook system—that is, loads are suspended from three different hook-up points—gives the Chinook the stability to carry heavy cargo, such as hulking 155-millimeter howitzers, at speeds exceeding 150 mph.

The cabin of the Chinook can accommodate two high-mobility multipurpose wheeled vehicles (Humvees) or a Humvee with a 105-millimeter howtizer and gun crew. The Chinook also can be configured for medical evacuation duties and can accommodate twenty-four stretchers.

The Chinook has undergone a series of upgrades since first being introduced in the 1960s. The latest versions include systems to reduce vibration and more powerful engines, along with automated flight controls. The Chinook is outfitted with jam-resistant

The massive CH-47 Chinook helicopters deployed artillery pieces, light vehicles, and squads of soldiers.

radio systems, helicopter mounts, and chaff and flare dispensers.

The CH-46

Similar to but smaller than the Chinook is the CH-46 helicopter, which is primarily a troop-ferrying vehicle, sometimes described as a flying bus, for the U.S. Marine Corps. The CH-46 is a medium-lift assault helicopter with a maximum takeoff weight of 24,300 pounds and a range of nearly 152 miles. Operated by a crew of five—a pilot, copilot, crew chief, and two aerial gunners— the CH-46 can carry fourteen troops. The CH-46 is designed to be highly maneuverable, an essential feature in a helicopter whose primary mission is to quickly drop off

or pick up troops from combat zones. The copter was first developed in the 1960s to meet the medium-lift needs of the marines in the Vietnam War, and it has been used with modifications ever since.

The CH-46 was used widely in the Iraq War to move troops quickly into combat positions and to extricate wounded soldiers, but its services occasionally extended to humanitarian purposes. For example, on the second day of the war a CH-46 set down in the Iraqi desert to pick up wounded. One of the wounded turned out to be an Iraqi girl who had been injured in a cooking accident before the war even began. After marines had captured a nearby oil facility, the girl's relatives sought them out, begging for treatment for the girl. However, the government of Kuwait, where the CH-46 was based, would not allow Iraqis into the country. So the commander of the copter decided to fly the girl to the USS *Saipan* in the Persian Gulf so she could receive proper medical treatment.

More often, missions to pick up wounded soldiers were extremely dangerous. Fox News correspondent Oliver L. North, traveling with U.S. forces, witnessed one such mission. As the CH-46 was landing, a rocket-propelled grenade whizzed past, narrowly missing the copter. As North recalls, marines on the ground detected where the grenade had come from and opened fire "in a furious fusillade. A machine gunner . . . is hammering away at the tree line, and the up-gun on an [assault amphibious vehicle] off to our right starts popping 40mm grenades into the same area."[16] Ultimately, the medical evacuation was successful.

Used to transport soldiers into and out of enemy territory, the Pave Low helicopter flies low to the ground to avoid radar detection.

Pave Low Copters

Another important transport helicopter utilized during Operation Iraqi Freedom was the Pave Low. The air force's Pave Low heavy-lift helicopter is the largest and most technologically advanced helicopter in the world. The Pave Low has terrain-following and terrain-avoidance radar on board, along with a forward-looking infrared sensor and a projected map display, all of which allow Pave Low crews to follow terrain contours, avoid obstacles, and undertake low-altitude missions.

Designed to perform long-range, low-altitude penetrations into enemy-controlled areas either to deliver to or extricate troops from combat zones, the Pave Low was converted for special operations use to allow operations at night and under adverse weather conditions. The Pave Low is a modified version of the HH-53 Super Jolly Green Giant,

a heavy-lift copter used extensively in the Vietnam War. The large helicopter is powered by twin turbofan engines and self-lubricating, all-metal main and tail rotors. It is flown by a crew consisting of two pilots and a navigator; if the mission is to rescue trapped or wounded soldiers, two rescue technicians will also be aboard.

Pave Lows were used during the Iraq War to insert soldiers and special operations forces into desired locations. For example, on March 18, 2003, three Pave Lows carrying Toyota pickup trucks loaded with army special operations forces landed in the deserts of southern Iraq. Although one Pave Low had a landing mishap and crashed, no one was injured and the special ops forces took off for Nasiriyah in the remaining two pickup trucks in a top-secret mission to link up with sympathetic Iraqis and pick targets for coalition bombing.

The Screaming Eagles

Individual helicopters can operate effectively either as attack vehicles or as troop carriers, but masses of helicopters form a much more potent and fearsome force. Such is the case with the army's legendary 101st Airborne Division, which was instrumental in the Iraq War.

The 101st was formed during World War II and quickly became known as the Screaming Eagles. Members of the original 101st were part of the landing invasion force in Normandy on D-day, and they fought all the way into Germany. By the time of the Iraq War, the nature of the

equipment utilized by the 101st had vastly changed. For example, the 101st boasted seventy Apache helicopters, in excess of one hundred Black Hawk helicopters, and some forty Chinooks. The division's air assets were used with great effect as the coalition entered Iraq from Kuwait and made a headlong dash toward Baghdad. The helicopters enabled the division to rapidly move troops to combat zones, provide close air support for troops engaged in battle, and transport needed equipment and supplies to troops.

Members of the 101st engaged in battles throughout the Iraq War and played a role in the attack on Saddam Hussein's sons, Uday and Qusay, on July 22, 2003. Joining special operations forces, members of the 101st surrounded a house in Mosul containing the men, considered next in line to Saddam as wanted war criminals, and ordered them to surrender. When they refused, the building was hammered with a variety of rockets, missiles, and gunfire, which ultimately killed both men.

Fixed-wing aircraft received the lion's share of publicity during the Iraq War, with the news media's focus on precision bombing by coalition jets. However, helicopters added an important element to the overall coalition attack, providing intense firepower in support of ground troops. Moreover, helicopters did what no other aircraft could do in rugged desert terrain, delivering troops to the ground and withdrawing injured soldiers from the battlefield in a theater of war without landing strips.

Fire from the Air: Shock and Awe

The planes and helicopters arrayed against the Iraqi military were impressive in their own right, but they would not have been nearly as effective in defeating the enemy without an array of highly sophisticated munitions that were designed to hit their targets with deadly accuracy. These precision munitions allowed coalition forces to concentrate massive firepower on important military targets as part of what became known as a shock-and-awe campaign. By demonstrating an ability to strike targets at will with overwhelming force, the coalition sought to dissuade Iraqi soldiers from continuing to fight. The Iraq War marked the first time in the history of warfare that the great bulk of munitions used were high-tech precision weapons, a result in part because the coalition forces were determined not only to limit the amount of civilian casualties but also to obliterate the Iraqi war machine.

The phrase *shock and awe* arose from a 1996 paper coauthored by a former navy commander named Harlan K. Ullman. The paper, written for the National Defense University, was titled, "Shock and Awe: Achieving Rapid Dominance." Referring to the writings of Sun-tzu, a fourth-century B.C. Chinese military thinker, Ullman wrote, "Since before Sun Tzu, generals have been tantalized and confounded by the elusive goal of destroying the adversary's will to resist before, during and after battle."[17] Arguing that the U.S. military had begun to rely on a strategy that emphasized the gradual destruction of enemy troops, Ullman said the United States should utilize its high-technology advantage to make enemies believe any resistance is futile. Ullman's paper heavily influenced the Pentagon and was a driving force in planning for the Iraq War.

From the start of the war to war's declared end on May 1, 2003, U.S. planes hit 18,898 targets. Of those, 1,799 were leadership or military command structure targets. Most of the targets hit, however, were

Improved Weaponry

The military is constantly working to make weaponry more efficient, accurate, and potent. An example is the dreaded Hellfire missile, which is utilized by army, navy, and marine planes and helicopters to defeat tanks, provide close air support to ground troops, engage in urban assaults, and even incapacitate ships at sea.

In 2002 the Defense Threat Reduction Agency asked the Naval Air Systems Command (NAVAIR) to make the Hellfire missile even more potent than it was before. The result, unveiled in Operation Iraqi Freedom, was a new Hellfire whose warhead is crafted in such a way as to extend the lethal effects of detonation. According to a naval press release dated July 23, 2003, and headlined, "NAVAIR Designs, Builds More Potent Hellfire Warhead," NAVAIR's job was to "increase the probability of personnel lethality or incapacitation." The release explained that the solution was to layer fluorinated aluminum powder between the warhead casing and the warhead's explosives. Detonation of the missile disperses the aluminum mixture, which burns: "The resultant sustained high pressure is extremely effective against enemy personnel and structures."

The new Hellfire warheads were praised by the military. According to the release, Pentagon spokesman lieutenant commander Donald Sewell said, "The weapons were employed the first night of [the war] with great success." Sewell went on to quote the U.S. Marine Corps aviator who was credited with being the first to use the new Hellfire in combat. According to Sewell, the aviator said, "That thing was awesome. I thought it was a 2,000-pound JDAM going off," a reference to the satellite-guided bombs dropped by coalition bombers.

This video still shows an MQ-1 Predator equipped with Hellfire missiles capable of piercing the armor of any tank.

Iraqi troops, their tanks, and their weapons; 15,592 targets hit, or 82 percent of the total, were Iraqi soldiers and their weapons systems. Two-thirds of all bombs dropped—19,948—were precision munitions. In contrast, only 10 percent of the bombs dropped in Operation Desert Storm in 1991 were precision munitions. On the first night of the war, only precision weapons were used, and U.S. and coalition forces directed some 3,000 smart bombs into the Iraqi capital of Baghdad alone. A total of 29,199 bombs were dropped on Iraqi targets during the active military phase of Operation Iraqi Freedom.

Bomb Basics

Generally speaking, bombs are relatively simple devices. A bomb is made up of explosive material encased in a hard metal shell. Bombs usually have tail fins to help stabilize their fall to the earth and fuses to ensure the weapon detonates properly. However, a dizzying array of bombs have been created to accomplish specific missions. For example, some bombs are created to penetrate hardened targets, and others are designed to detonate in such a way as to send showers of deadly shrapnel into enemy positions.

The cheapest and simplest of bombs are the gravity bombs, those without an active guidance system. These bombs are dropped from planes and simply fall to the earth. How much damage they inflict against the enemy is a matter of skill, luck, wind currents, and other factors beyond the bomber's control.

These bombs also produce the most chance of what the military calls "collateral damage"—that is, the destruction of nonmilitary facilities and civilian casualties.

Because of the military's desire to limit collateral damage, precision weapons, so-called smart bombs, were used extensively in the Iraq War. In general, smart bombs are simply gravity bombs that have been modified. Modifications usually include an electronic sensor system, a computer to act as a control system, and adjustable flight fins. When dropped, the smart bomb becomes similar to a glider airplane. Although it does not have a propulsion system, as is found in missiles, it gains forward momentum simply by virtue of having been dropped from a plane. Flight fins help stabilize the bomb's flight to the earth, while the computer and adjustable fins allow the bomb to steer itself. The electronic sensor provides the computer with information about the location of the target, and the computer processes the information to calculate how the bomb should turn in order to hit the intended target.

Once those calculations have been processed, the computer orders actuators to adjust the bomb's flight fins. These fins are similar to flaps on an airplane wing. Tilting the fins in a given direction creates drag, allowing the bomb to turn. The sensors on the smart bombs provide continuous information to the computer, which constantly makes flight adjustments until the bomb hits its target and explodes.

Joint Directional Attack Munitions

One of the most used and widely discussed weapons in the coalition arsenal during Operation Iraqi Freedom was the joint directional attack munition (JDAM). JDAMs are essentially "dumb" gravity bombs that have been converted with kits into precision-guided "smart" bombs. The tail section of the kit contains an inertial navigational system, a computer to process and serve as a control center, and a sophisticated global positioning system (GPS). Use of the kits improves the accuracy of bombs in any weather condition. The military uses the kits to create JDAMs with the two-thousand-pound BLU-109 and the MK-84 bombs and with the one-thousand-pound BLU-110 and MK-83 bombs.

Navy crewmen inspect JDAM bombs before loading them onto awaiting aircraft.

JDAMs are relatively cheap—only eighteen thousand dollars per kit—but assembling smart bombs can be labor intensive and time consuming. "It takes a team of eight people an average of about two hours to build a load of 12 JDAMs,"[18] says air force tech sergeant Mike Potratz. The starting point in creation of a JDAM is a one-thousand- or two-thousand-pound dumb bomb. A fuse, fin kit, sensor, and other components are assembled and attached to the bomb, turning it into the precision JDAM.

Although the work can be tedious, munitions specialists making the JDAMs believed they were part of a larger team that would help bring victory. "Putting bombs on target is the aircrew's ultimate mission, and without Ammo troops, there's no mission,"[19] Potratz says.

JDAMs are guided by satellite technology. The pilot enters the target's coordinates into the bomb's satellite receiver, and when released the bomb hones in on the programmed target. The JDAM's satellite system tracks the target information relative to the bomb's position—information processed by the onboard computer—which directs the control system to adjust the bomb's flight fins to steer it toward its target. JDAMs proved particularly valuable because they can find their targets even in blinding sandstorms—a major issue in the deserts of Iraq. The air force says 6,642 JDAMs were dropped on Iraq during the war, and they were stunningly accurate, often falling within ten feet of their intended targets. (According to the air force, another 4,590 GPS-guided smart bombs were used in the Iraq War, but they cost significantly more than JDAMs.)

A massive ordnance air-blast bomb is a satellite-guided weapon packed with over eighteen thousand pounds of explosives.

On March 21, 2003, sailors aboard the USS *Harry S. Truman* engaged in a richly choreographed routine as aviation ordnancemen in their distinctive red jerseys readied JDAMs to be loaded onto planes aboard the aircraft carrier for the opening salvo of Operation Iraqi Freedom. "We train the way we fight," said Aviation Ordnanceman First Class Rob Upton. "We're prepared for this. It feels good knowing that we're going to do what we've been trained to do . . . that we're going to be able to use it now. We're going to make a difference in whatever actions are taken."[20]

Laser-Guided Bombs

Although JDAMs received the lion's share of publicity, the bulk of smart weaponry unleashed on Iraqi forces utilized technology dating back to the 1991 Gulf War. These bombs were laser-guided weapons that, under the correct conditions, can be highly accurate. However, environmental conditions can cause the bombs to go off course. For example, the laser beam can be deflected by such things as dust, smoke, rain, and even humidity. In order to be effective, contact between the bomb's laser sensors and the target must not be interrupted. To operate, a laser beam is focused on a target, and sensors—photo diodes sensitive to laser light—in the bomb follow the laser. The high-intensity laser can be beamed on a target either by a soldier on the ground or by an aviator in the plane dropping the bomb. The laser bounces off the target, and the sensors in the bomb pick up the beam and follow it.

Because a host of bombs can be in the air at any given time, intended for varying targets, unique laser pulse patterns are used. Before a bomb is dropped, the aircraft computer links with the bomb's control system to establish the pulse pattern that will be used. Once the bomb is dropped, its control system only picks up laser energy with that unique pulse pattern. The laser-guided weapons are much more expensive than JDAMs, costing roughly one hundred thousand dollars apiece. Nevertheless, nearly 40 percent of the smart bombs dropped in the Iraq War were laser guided.

Although smart bombs garnered the most interest, the military found that gravity, or dumb, bombs could still play a role. A total of 9,251 gravity bombs, nearly a third of the total, were used during Operation Iraqi Freedom, mostly in circumstances in which the risk of civilian casualties or damage to nonmilitary property was minimal.

Super Bombs

The U.S. military has developed a number of nonnuclear "super bombs" capable of inflicting massive destruction. Their existence alone is said to have a powerful deterrent effect on enemy troops. The United States took advantage of the super bomb's reputation—none was used in the Iraq War, but military officials publicly announced that the weapons had been delivered to the theater for use if necessary. One such super bomb is the BLU-82, or Daisy Cutter, which was used in the war in Afghanistan against the Taliban. Weighing 15,000 pounds, the bomb is so large that it has to be dropped from a cargo plane. Until Operation Iraqi Freedom, the Daisy Cutter was the largest nonnuclear bomb on the planet. It is nearly twelve feet long and about four and a half feet in diameter, housing 12,600 pounds of ammonium nitrate and aluminum powder that, when detonated, creates a uniquely unnerving explosion because it is so loud. Indeed, the bomb's noise upon detonation is nearly as effective against enemy troops as the actual damage it inflicts. The psychological impact on enemy troops can often lead to mass surrenders even when the weapon misses its target.

The next major development of nonnuclear super bombs came with creation of the massive ordnance air-blast bomb (MOAB). The bomb has been nicknamed "the Mother of All Bombs," a play on Saddam Hussein's promise during the Gulf War for a "Mother of All Battles" against coalition troops. The MOAB is a 21,700-pound bomb that contains 18,700 pounds of high explosive. The bomb is thirty feet long, and unlike the Daisy Cutter, it is guided by satellite—meaning the bomb is not only highly destructive but also highly accurate.

Hellfire Missiles

In addition to bombs, the coalition arsenal included a variety of missiles that provided the military with operational flexibility and devastating firepower. A prime example is the Hellfire missile.

The Hellfire is an air-to-ground precision munition designed for use against tanks and other armored vehicles. Although there are several versions of the Hellfire in use by the military, the missiles generally can be said to be laser-guided weapons that seek out laser beams and follow them to their designated targets. A newer generation of Hellfire missile hones in on radar frequencies. Utilized by the navy, air force, and marines, the Hellfire missile is powered by a single-stage motor that can reach speeds of 950 miles per hour.

Two basic techniques are utilized to deliver the Hellfire missile to its target. In the so-called autonomous method, operators on board the plane or helicopter firing the missile guide it by laser all the way to its intended target. The other primary means of delivering the missile is the remote method, in which the aircraft releases the missile in the general vicinity of the target, and operators in another aircraft or on the ground guide the missile to the target with a laser beam. The remote method offers the advantage of allowing the attacking aircraft to remain at a relatively safe distance from enemy forces. However, it also requires a high degree of coordination between the attacking craft and spotters. Among other craft, the Hellfire is utilized by the Apache and Cobra helicopters as well as by the A-10 Warthog plane.

Another laser-guided air-to-ground missile in use by the military is the Maverick missile. Effective against tanks, armored vehicles, and bunkers, the Maverick can be fitted with either of two types of warheads. One has a fuse that detonates on contact with its target. The other is a heavyweight warhead that has a delayed fuse, allowing the missile to penetrate its target prior to exploding. This missile is especially effective against hardened targets, such as bunkers. The Maverick is propelled by a solid-rocket motor. The speed of the missile is classified information, but it is known that each missile weighs about three hundred pounds and costs some $180,000.

Targeting

Whether guided by lasers or satellites, the precision munitions utilized by the coalition forces during the Iraq War helped the United States and its allies in their goal of minimizing civilian casualties and other collateral damage. However, the use of smart bombs was not enough by itself. Several teams within

the Combined Air Operations Center worked to make sure the coalition was able to achieve its war aims while at the same time reducing the risk of civilian deaths. What that meant from a practical standpoint is that cultural, historic, religious, and medical buildings were not attacked unless Iraqi troops were using them to conduct military operations. Even then, extraordinary measures were taken to minimize the risks to noncombatants and nonmilitary property. "Even though our top goal is to take out the desired target, our primary concern and bottom line is to . . . avoid at all costs, any type of civilian casualties," said Master Sergeant Douglas Frickey, a leader of the Time-Sensitive Targeting (TST) team. "We've been practicing, exercising and refining our efforts regarding collateral damage estimation for the past

Cluster Bombs

Cluster bombs are highly efficient, highly lethal weapons that allow both air- and ground-based bombers to destroy airfields and surface-to-air missile sites. These relatively large bombs open in midair, scattering hundreds of smaller bomblets over a broad area. The bomblets are supposed to explode on impact, but any given cluster bomb can produce a wide number of so-called duds.

These duds lay on the ground and can maim or kill someone who touches them. Lying like mines on the surface of the ground, the bomblets have bright coloring that make them attractive to children, many of whom have been killed or seriously injured by picking up cluster weapons that failed to explode on impact. Thus, cluster bombs are highly controversial because, unlike precision-

guided weapons, they disperse their explosives over a broad area and their remnants cannot all be accounted for.

According to Human Rights Watch, a global organization dedicated to protecting human rights, the United States and the United Kingdom used nearly 13,000 cluster munitions in Operation Iraqi Freedom, which, combined, contained up to 2 millon bomblets. A Human Rights Watch special report by Steve Goose, "Cluster Munitions: Toward a Global Solution," found that "cluster munition strikes, particularly ground attacks on populated areas, were a major cause of civilian casualties; hospital records show cluster strikes caused hundreds of civilian deaths and injuries in Baghdad, al-Hilla, al-Najaf, Basra, and elsewhere."

Maverick Guided Missiles

The Maverick guided missile is a significant weapon utilized by the U.S. Air Force, Marine Corps, and Navy to provide close air support for troops and destroy tactical targets on the battlefield. Originally developed as a laser-guided

weapon, newer versions of the Maverick are heat-seeking, allowing the weapons to be used at night or in bad weather.

The missiles are particularly useful to pilots because they have what is known as a "launch-and-leave" capability. Once a pilot selects a target, locks on to it, and fires the weapon, he can leave the area or select another target. The launch-and-leave feature is distinguished from other laser-guided weaponry in which operators must continue to lock a laser beam on a target until the weapon hits its target.

The Maverick is eight feet, two inches long and weighs between 462 and 670 pounds, depending on the model and weight of the warhead. The navy, for example, uses a 300-pound penetrating warhead, whereas the marines and air force use a 125-pound warhead.

A British pilot inspects a Maverick guided missile under the wing of his Harrier fighter-bomber.

decade. During the current air campaign, we are now adding practical experience to further hone our skills."[21]

To determine the potential for collateral damage, members of the Time-Sensitive Targeting team used a high-tech computer program based on mathematical probability theories and hypothetical scenarios. Members were able to test on the computer program the impact of different weapons on such targets and determine the amount of collateral damage that could be expected from such strikes.

Whenever a potential target was identified that held the potential for collateral damage, team members analyzed the risk and reported to superiors. The reports were sent up the chain of command, and they sometimes made it all the way up to Secretary of Defense Donald Rumsfeld. Rumsfeld reviewed reports relating to targets that, if struck, posed a high risk of high-collateral damage. High-collateral damage was defined by the military as attacks that could result in the deaths of thirty or more civilians or have a significant negative effect on a particular site ordinarily on the protected list, such as a culturally significant structure. On March 30 Rumsfeld said at a press conference, "We are very concerned about human life, particularly ours, but also other human life, innocent. Think of the Iraqi people not as warriors against the West. These are hostages to a vicious regime. It's important that we win, and we will win, but it's also important how we win."[22]

The TST team put in long hours during Operation Iraqi Freedom. At the beginning of the conflict, when almost two thousand attack missions were being flown daily, members of the team were calculating potential damage estimates twenty-four hours a day. "With our forces moving so quickly, we were providing collateral damage estimation information around the clock," Frickey says. "We like to think that every call we make on a target has the same high importance, and that importance is to hit the target and make sure there are no civilians hurt."[23]

Weather Forecasting

In addition to worrying about the potential for inadvertently striking civilians or damaging buildings not related to the Iraqi military's war effort, planners of the air campaign in Operation Iraqi Freedom also had to keep a close eye on weather conditions. While many of the military's newest planes and weapons can be utilized in nearly any weather conditions, bad weather could affect the safety of takeoffs and landings. And on missions using laser-guided weaponry,

weather also could play a role in the ultimate success of the attack. Indeed, bad weather on one day could have an effect on operations and missions the next, particularly if planes had to be redirected to land at alternate bases.

Pilots utilizing the latest in satellite-guided bombs could successfully deliver their bombs to their intended targets in poor weather. However, strong storms or blowing sandstorms at the pilots' home bases could cause them to have to land at other bases. Consequently, those pilots and their planes might not be available for use in some future missions. "Even though the weather may not be a factor over the target area, somewhere in . . . [the] process it always is,"[24] says Lieutenant Colonel Fred Fahlbusch, the Combined Air Operations Center's weather cell chief. Even humanitarian and propaganda flights could be influenced by weather conditions. For example, pilots need to know wind conditions at drop zones when airdropping humanitarian food supplies because strong winds could cause the aid to drift far from its intended target, rendering it useless to civilians. Likewise, pilots dropping leaflets urging Iraqi soldiers to surrender also needed to know wind conditions to ensure the leaflets fell where Iraqi soldiers could read them.

Members of the weather team played a key part in development of a day's bombing campaign. In addition to providing weather information—ranging from forecasts to current conditions—to bombing planners, the team also kept abreast of weather conditions at planned aerial refueling locations. The information was invaluable to bombing planners, who could use it to decide what types of weapons to use against specific targets.

Even as the military's weather experts labored to keep abreast of weather to limit the impact of poor conditions on coalition bombing runs, they likewise looked for ways to exploit the weather as an additional weapon against the Iraqis. For example, if weather forecasters knew that Iraqi airfields in a target area were shrouded in severe sandstorms, they could reasonably assume that Iraqi fighter jets would not scramble to intercept coalition bombers. "We use adverse weather to our advantage because if they can't fly, then they can't take off and come at us,"[25] says Fahlbusch. Although the Iraqi air force apparently decided it was grossly outmatched and never got its planes airborne during the conflict, weather forecasters were nevertheless major contributors to the war effort. As just one example, they monitored conditions at planned aerial refueling areas. If the area was going to be saturated with clouds, thunderstorms, or ice, the weather team recommended an alternate site.

The coalition utilized a wide array of sophisticated and precise munitions that by and large were able to isolate the Iraqi military while avoiding substantial numbers of casualties among Iraqi citizens. Some of the weapons in the coalition arsenal, such as sophisticated weather forecasting tools, were not intended to hurt the Iraqi military but rather to make other weapons more effective. Use of deadly accurate munitions sigificantly softened the resistance of Iraqi soldiers, paving the way for a steady advance of ground troops.

Chapter 5

Ground War Weapons: "The Baghdad Urban Renewal Project"

The U.S.-led coalition military force dominated Iraq from the air in clear technological superiority. However, airpower and sophisticated missiles alone were not enough to achieve the Bush administration's goal of driving Saddam Hussein from power and uncovering Iraq's alleged arsenal of weapons of mass destruction. As in any war, victory hinged on having troops on the ground to secure and occupy territory, and the U.S. troops went into the Iraq War as perhaps the best-equipped fighters in the history of warfare.

The speed of the ground offensive by coalition troops was breathtaking. Ground forces entered Iraq and began a virtual sprint toward the capital of Baghdad, advancing in armored columns that covered some one hundred miles during the first day of operations. Along the way, ground troops seized key airfields, took prisoners, and secured oil fields and dams. Dozens of small special operations forces armed with high-technology tools disrupted Iraqi command and control systems, including communications systems, acts of sabotage intended to hasten the collapse of Iraqi forces. Unlike bombs dropped from the air, which Iraqi leaders and troops could potentially escape by burrowing into bunkers, ground troops provided a constant, tangible threat that quickly became a victorious juggernaut.

Protective Armor

Although ground troops are most often thought of in their capacity as attacking forces, one of the most important pieces of equipment for the modern soldier is his or her protective armor. Today's foot soldier is encased in protective clothing designed to offer protection from enemy attack without restricting mobility. Lightweight, flameproof, chemical resistant, and able to deflect bullets, shrapnel, and knives, modern protective gear allows today's soldier almost unfettered mobility and a high degree of safety.

The modern Kevlar helmet weighs less and offers better protection than the steel helmets once worn by American combat troops.

As the war in Iraq began, most soldiers were outfitted with a roughly 25-pound vest made of Kevlar weave that provided a high degree of protection against enemy weapons. Known as the personal armor system, ground troops (PASGT), the body armor included a lightweight Kevlar helmet (about 3 pounds) and vest. However, an improved version, also made of Kevlar weave, was introduced during the conflict and was shipped to troops in the field. This new vest weighed just 16.4 pounds, yet it could stop 9-millimeter ammunition. The vest came with removable throat and groin protectors and inserts made of a tough ceramic that could block 7.62-millimeter ammunition.

Great strides have been made in the development of increasingly effective yet light-weight body armor. In the 1960s soldiers wore nylon "flak" vests and steel helmets. In the 1980s the Kevlar-based PASGT was introduced. Although the gear's effectiveness was increased with the switch, it weighed about the same as its 1960s predecessor. During the 1990s an improved Kevlar product lightened the vest and increased the protection it provided.

Ongoing Improvement

The special body armor worn by troops in Operation Iraqi Freedom was credited by military officials as saving numerous lives with its bullet- and shrapnel-halting ability. Nevertheless, specialists continued to work to bring further improvements to body armor. An ongoing project by the army seeks to reduce the weight of the protective gear even more.

Protective gear, water, ammunition, and weapons make up the bulk of the weight soldiers must carry. "The Army is putting the best available armor materials into soldiers' armor," according to Philip Cuniff, a research mechanical engineer with the Ballistics Technology Team at the U.S. Army Soldier Systems Center in Natick, Massachusetts. "Part of our work in the Ballistics Technology Team is to develop new materials and techniques to lighten the load of those armor systems."[26] The researchers are working with fibers such as Zylon, first developed by the air force in the 1980s, to develop a new generation of body armor. Prototype helmets weigh less than two pounds and provide the same level of protection as the current Kevlar version.

Vests and helmets were not the only protective gear worn by troops. Soldiers also were equipped with chemical protection suits that included gloves and overboots, along with gas masks, for use in case of a chemical or biological attack by the Iraqis. The gear was especially important because certain types of nerve agents can be deadly even with minimal skin contact. Though the suits were hot and uncomfortable, they provided the only foolproof protection in the event of a chemical or biological attack. Consequently, any time the Iraqis launched

Scud missiles in the vicinity of U.S. troops, special alarms had troops scrambling to put on their protective gear. Just as in the 1991 Gulf War, the Iraqis did not use chemical or biological weapons. However, when U.S. forces found a cache of Iraqi chemical suits, coalition officials feared the worst and prepared accordingly.

Combat Gear

In addition to protective gear, the modern U.S. soldier also goes into combat with a variety of gear intended to improve his or her effectiveness against the enemy. Ranging from basic utility items such as flashlights to high-tech handheld satellite positioning devices, the gear carried by soldiers in Operation Iraqi Freedom allowed them to be ready for any contingency.

One technological advantage held by U.S. ground troops over their Iraqi counterparts was the ability to engage in nighttime operations. Night-vision goggles made such operations possible, allowing soldiers to see in almost total darkness. Night-vision systems could be carried by soldiers or attached to their helmets. The units contain an image-intensifier tube that amplifies available light, such as that from stars. Binocular eyepieces allow soldiers to see their surroundings as clearly as if in daylight, albeit in green shades. When no light is available, soldiers can make use of an infrared light feature in the goggles. Invisible to the naked eye, the infrared light can be seen by the goggles, again allowing users to see as clearly as at midday. Night-vision goggles weigh just a bit over one pound and operate on batteries that can last up to forty hours.

Rifles

Soldiers, of course, require offensive weapons. And just like their counterparts in warfare as far back as the fourteenth century, soldiers in Operation Iraqi Freedom relied on a long-barreled firearm, but the rifles of the Iraq War bore little resemblance to the weapons of the 1300s.

The infantrymen of the Vietnam War relied on the feared M-16 rifle, which was capable of firing up to 950 bullets a minute at a range of some thirteen hundred feet. In 1994 the army switched to a variation of the M-16 known as the M4 carbine, which was used in Operation Iraqi Freedom. A carbine is a rifle whose barrel has been shortened. The M4 fires 5.56-millimeter bullets and can shoot three bullets with each trigger pull. The M4 weighs just 5.5 pounds and is roughly thirty inches long, and it can accurately hit targets close to two thousand feet away.

Infantrymen in Iraq also had other weapons they could bring to bear against their Iraqi counterparts. The M67 frag-

U.S. soldiers secure a Baghdad marketplace with M4 carbines and a vehicle-mounted light machine gun.

mentation grenade, for example, weighs just fourteen ounces. However, when it explodes, it is lethal within fifteen feet and capable of inflicting serious injury within a radius of nearly fifty feet. (Fragments disperse as much as seven hundred feet.)

The Patriot

One important tool of coalition forces had both defensive and offensive properties. The Patriot missile air defense system helped to protect soldiers from Iraqi missile launches. Maligned for its so-so performance in Operation Desert Storm, the Patriot missile system generally drew high marks for its effectiveness in Operation Iraqi Freedom.

The Patriot is a long-range, all-altitude, all-weather air defense system. It contains a high-explosive ninety kilogram warhead that destroys incoming missiles in midair. Patriots successfully destroyed many Iraqi missiles by utilizing new guidance-enhanced missiles that allowed for midcourse corrections from a mobile engagement control center.

The Patriot system was originally designed as an antiaircraft weapon before being redesigned to shoot down missiles. After successful testing, the Patriot was first used in combat during Operation Desert Storm. Military officials originally claimed great successes for the Patriot, but it later became apparent that the system had been largely ineffective in intercepting Iraqi missiles. The revised Patriot system is able to protect a much larger area than the original missile defense system, providing security for an area about seven times greater.

The redesigned Patriot enjoyed much greater success in Operation Iraqi Freedom, providing soldiers with both peace of mind and real security.

Bradley Fighting Vehicles

Not usually thought of as a weapon, the Bradley fighting vehicle was an important element in U.S. ground soldiers' equipment during Operation Iraqi Freedom. Resembling a small tank in appearance, the Bradley is a tracked, armored vehicle used to transport soldiers on the battlefield, provide fire cover for troops on the ground, and engage enemy tanks and troop transport vehicles. Bradleys are manned by a commander, gunner, and driver and can accommodate six fully equipped infantry soldiers. The Bradley replaced the M113 vehicle, which was, in essence, a battle taxi capable only of transporting troops to the battlefield. By contrast, the Bradley packs significant firepower and is capable of destroying any enemy armored vehicle it encounters.

The Bradley is equipped with an M242 chain gun, which has a single barrel capable of firing between two hundred and five hundred shots a minute. The M242 can fire a variety of ammunition, including armor-piercing munitions and high-explosive ammunition. In addition, the Bradley has a 7.62-millimeter machine gun. When taking on heavy tanks, the Bradley relies on a tube-launched, optically tracked, wire-guided (TOW) antitank missile system. The wings and tail fins of these missiles are folded inside its body until it is launched

The Bradley Fighting Vehicle

It looks like a minitank. And although its primary mission is to transport infantry troops on the battlefied, the Bradley fighting vehicle packs significant firepower of its own.

The fully armored Bradley has medium- and long-range firepower through its M242 25-millimeter "Bushmaster" chain gun, which can fire either armor-piercing or high-explosive ammunition. The Bradley also has TOW antitank missiles on board.

Consequently, the Bradley is a far cry from the old M113 vehicles that it replaced, which essentially were battle taxis designed to ferry troops to the fighting. Indeed, during Operation Desert Storm more enemy armored vehicles were destroyed by Bradley fighting vehicles than by Abrams tanks.

The Bradley continued its legacy during Operation Iraqi Freedom, providing added firepower to the coalition ground assault. The vehicle's armor also protected untold numbers of infantry soldiers from Iraqi fire, making it a versatile cog in the coalition war machine.

The Bradley fighting vehicle is equipped with less armor and smaller caliber weapons than a main battle tank.

from a smooth tube launcher located on the vehicle's turret. The TOW has a high-explosive warhead and is powered by a two-stage solid propellant motor that can reach speeds approaching the speed of sound. The TOW can knock out any armored vehicle in the world.

In addition to its offensive weaponry, the Bradley also is equipped with devices intended to baffle enemy munitions. For example, the Bradley fighting vehicle has two smoke grenade dischargers as well as an engine smoke–generating system, which can obscure the vehicle and make it difficult for enemy forces to use laser-guided missiles against them. Bradley fighting vehicles are amphibious, and their six hundred horsepower enables them to keep pace with U.S. tanks. The Bradley weighs fifty thousand pounds and can travel at speeds of up to forty-five miles per hour. A Bradley can travel three hundred miles on a tank of gas.

Humvees

Another important vehicle for ground troops is the high-mobility multipurpose wheeled vehicle, perhaps better known by its nickname of Humvee. The light, mobile, four-wheel-drive vehicle serves a variety of purposes for the military, ranging from a troop carrier to an ambulance. The Humvee replaced the quarter-ton jeep in the Gulf War. Fifteen feet long by a little over seven feet wide, the Humvee weighs fifty-two hundred pounds. It is powered by a diesel engine and is equipped with an automatic transmission and four-wheel drive. The Humvee can travel 350 miles on a tank of gas and can travel at speeds of up to sixty-five miles per hour.

A Humvee can be airlifted and parachuted to the ground in support of ground troops, and it is considered the world's premiere light military truck. Humvees come in a variety of configurations, designed to meet specialized needs. For example, one

model is designed to carry a two-man crew and eight troops and has no external armament. Another model is armored and has a weapon mount on the vehicle's roof. Still other versions of the Humvee are designed for use as field ambulances, capable of carrying between two and twelve patients.

In all, the Humvee can be configured to serve a variety of functions for the military. Humvees are used as cargo carriers, troop transport vehicles, armament carriers, TOW missile system carriers, shelter carriers, and ambulances.

Abrams Tanks

Perhaps the premiere fighting vehicle in the U.S. inventory is the M-1 A1/2 Abrams tank. Operated by a crew of four—a commander, gunner, ammunition loader, and driver—the Abrams packs an enormous punch. The tank is outfitted with three machine guns, a 12.7-millimeter Browning M2 machine gun and two 7.62-millimeter M240 machine guns. The tank's main gun is a 120-millimeter MW56 smoothbore gun. This gun, which protrudes from the tank's turret, is highly accurate even when the tank is in motion and traveling over rough terrain. It is capable of firing a wide range of ammunition, including rounds that include armor-piercing penetrators made of depleted uranium, a militarily useful material because its density enables it to pierce the thickest armor of enemy tanks. Depleted uranium has a density that is more than twice that of ordinary steel.

Inside the Abrams

The Abrams tank is a marvel of firepower and provides excellent protection for its crew. However, that does not mean the Abrams is particularly comfortable.

U.S. Army E-4 specialist Darrell Smith recalled his experiences in Operation Iraqi Freedom to Indiana's *Linton Daily Citizen* when home on a rest-and-relaxation leave. Smith said he and his four-man tank crew found themselves day after day in a cramped, hot space for hours at a time. Smith said it was not unusual for temperatures inside the tank to hit the 150-degree mark by 7 A.M.

Nevertheless, Smith said the tank saved his life. Armed with a 120-millimeter cannon, two 7.62-millimeter machine guns, a 50-caliber gun, and two carbines, the tank provided more than ample protection against the Iraqis arrayed against them.

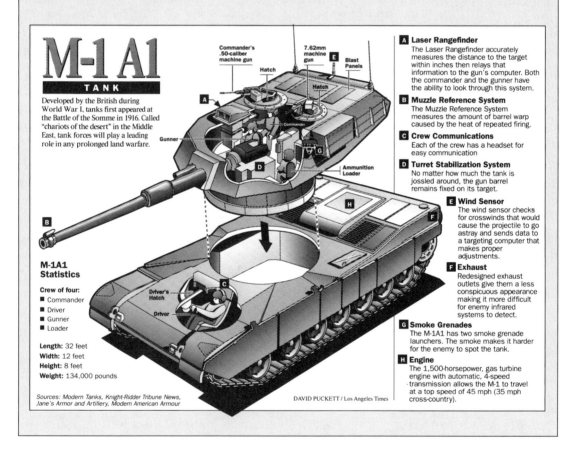

M-1 A1 TANK

Developed by the British during World War I, tanks first appeared at the Battle of the Somme in 1916. Called "chariots of the desert" in the Middle East, tank forces will play a leading role in any prolonged land warfare.

Commander's .50-caliber machine gun
7.62mm machine gun
Blast Panels
Hatch
Hatch
Gunner
Commander
Ammunition Loader

M-1A1 Statistics

Crew of four:
- Commander
- Driver
- Gunner
- Loader

Length: 32 feet
Width: 12 feet
Height: 8 feet
Weight: 134,000 pounds

Driver's Hatch
Driver

Sources: Modern Tanks, Knight-Ridder Tribune News, Jane's Armor and Artillery, Modern American Armour

DAVID PUCKETT / Los Angeles Times

A Laser Rangefinder
The Laser Rangefinder accurately measures the distance to the target within inches then relays that information to the gun's computer. Both the commander and the gunner have the ability to look through this system.

B Muzzle Reference System
The Muzzle Reference System measures the amount of barrel warp caused by the heat of repeated firing.

C Crew Communications
Each of the crew has a headset for easy communication

D Turret Stabilization System
No matter how much the tank is jossled around, the gun barrel remains fixed on its target.

E Wind Sensor
The wind sensor checks for crosswinds that would cause the projectile to go astray and sends data to a targeting computer that makes proper adjustments.

F Exhaust
Redesigned exhaust outlets give them a less conspicuous appearance making it more difficult for enemy infrared systems to detect.

G Smoke Grenades
The M-1A1 has two smoke grenade launchers. The smoke makes it harder for the enemy to spot the tank.

H Engine
The 1,500-horsepower, gas turbine engine with automatic, 4-speed transmission allows the M-1 to travel at a top speed of 45 mph (35 mph cross-country).

The depleted uranium rounds have proven extemely effective against other tanks and hardened targets such as bunkers, and they were used extensively in Operation Iraqi Freedom, with U.S. and British forces using between 1,100 and

2,200 tons of depleted uranium rounds during attacks in Iraq during March and April 2003. By contrast, an estimated 375 tons of depleted uranium munitions were used during Operation Desert Storm. While the Pentagon has downplayed the risks of depleted uranium use—depleted uranium is both toxic and slightly radioactive—others are not so certain.

In June 2003 the *Seattle Post-Intelligencer* tested six sites in Iraq and found elevated levels of radiation at all of them. At one site—an Iraqi tank bombed by a depleted uranium munition—radiation levels were fifteen hundred times higher than normal background radiation. Scientists and physicians worry about the potential for a significant increase in the number of cancer cases in Iraq as a result of the use of depleted uranium munitions.

Nevertheless, depleted uranium products are also used to provide protection for troops. The heavily armored Abrams tank has steel-encased depleted uranium armor, and armor also separates the crew compartment from the vehicle's fuel tanks and ammunition compartments. The tank's top portion is designed to blow outward when hit by enemy muntions, a feature intended to save the lives of tank crewmen.

Abrams Features

In addition to heavy armor, the Abrams provides other features to protect the safety of its occupants. A clean-air ventilation system provides protection against nuclear, biological, and chemical threats, and sensors aboard the tank also monitor the air for the presence of radiological or chemical agents. Tank crews also wear protective suits and masks.

Unlike a car or a Humvee, a tank does not have windows. Consequently, a tank in many respects resembles a land-based submarine. The Abrams is equipped with a variety of periscopes that allow its operators to achieve a panoramic view of their surroundings in either daylight or nighttime conditions. The driver's station, located at the center of the tank's hull, is equipped with three periscopes, providing the driver with a 120-degree field of vision. The commander's tank station has six periscopes that allow a 360-degree view. In addition, the commander's station is equipped to allow the commander to fire the tank's main gun independent of the crew's gunner. The crew's gunner has special sights, including a thermal-imaging system for nighttime operations. In this system, an image is created based on the differences in heat radiated by objects on the battlefield. These images are displayed on the eyepiece of the gunner's sight, and they are integrated with readings from a laser range finder aboard the tank. A sophisticated computer aboard the Abrams also analyzes a variety of data, including wind, barometric pressure, ammunition type, and temperature, to determine the proper gun angle to hit a given target.

Weighing more than sixty tons, the Abrams is nevertheless capable of speeds of up to 45 miles per hour. The tank contains a fifteen hundred horsepower Lycoming

Where Did They Go?

During Operation Desert Storm in 1991, coalition forces found that they were often inundated with mass surrenders of Iraqi troops. However, mass surrenders were uncommon during Operation Iraqi Freedom.

At a press briefing on March 23, 2003, a reporter asked Lieutenant General John Abizaid why there were so few surrenders by Iraqis despite the coalition's overwhelming firepower advantage. Abizaid's reply is found at the U.S. Central Command Web site:

> I think the main reason that there haven't been a lot of mass surrenders on the same scale as in 1991 is that the Iraqi forces really were trapped in Kuwait. They were far away from home. They had nowhere to melt back to. Here in the areas that we've been encountering regular Iraqi forces, by far the majority of units have just melted away. We find a substantial amount of abandoned equipment on the field, and in the regular army there is clearly very, very little will to fight. True, we've captured 2,000 prisoners thus far, but the units that we have expected to find in various locations and put up resistance really haven't done so.

Textron gas turbine engine and has four forward and two reverse gears. The Abrams can travel about 275 miles on a tank of gas.

Nonlethal Weapons

In addition to weapons of incredible lethality, coalition forces also utilized nonlethal weapons during Operation Iraqi Freedom. One such weapon was used by ground forces and is intended to help disperse hostile crowds and ward off enemy combatants. The weapon, called a long-range acoustic device, blasts earsplitting noise in a directed beam. It was originally developed as a nonlethal weapon after the terrorist attack on the USS *Cole* in Yemen in a bid to keep small ships from approaching U.S. warships. The weapon was then picked up by the U.S. Army and U.S. Marine Corps, which used it in Baghdad and other areas during Operation Iraqi Freedom.

Despite the lethal firepower at their disposal and high-technology devices to make their weapons more effective, perhaps the most important weapon available to U.S. soldiers was confidence. Prior to the war, a marine Cobra pilot from Marine Light Attack Helicopter Squadron 267 said Iraqi soldiers would be well advised to surrender if they encountered him because, "if he points a gun at me, he's dead."[27] As Oliver North noted in his book *War Stories,* some soldiers began to jokingly refer to the coming war as "the Baghdad Urban Renewal Project."[28]

Coalition forces used a wide array of weaponry in its ground-war campaign against Iraqi forces. Ranging from modern rifles and high-technology night-vision goggles to low-technology leaflets, the weapons used in Operation Iraqi Freedom all had one common goal: to help bring the conflict to a quick and successful resolution. Despite all the firepower the coalition was able to bring to the war, however, its effectiveness would have been minimized if not for accurate intelligence about the location of Iraqi troops and the size of those troop concentrations.

Chapter 6

Surveillance

The United States and its coalition partners enjoyed an unquestioned advantage in weaponry over Iraq. However, sophisticated weapons by themselves would have been ineffective if not for detailed intelligence that allowed planners to target bombing missions and ground assaults. Utilizing information gleaned from satellites, sophisticated planes, pilotless drones, and special operations forces on the ground, the coalition enjoyed a clear picture of the battlefield—another enormous advantage over the Iraqi military.

Operation Iraqi Freedom used 40 percent fewer troops than were used in the 1991 Gulf War, thanks in part to the increased use of space-age technology. Satellites in the global positioning system (GPS), for example, allowed bombers to drop fifty-five hundred GPS-guided joint directional attack munitions (JDAMs) with pinpoint accuracy, most within roughly ten feet of their intended targets.

Another fifty satellites allowed for unfettered communications, surveillance, and weather forecasting.

The U.S. government and military have long recognized the potential and importance of outer space in armed conflict. After the Soviet Union became the first nation to successfully launch an earth satellite, many American leaders feared that satellites ultimately could provide a platform for military domination. The Senate majority leader at the time, Lyndon B. Johnson, warned that the United States could not afford the luxury of shrugging off the Soviet Union's success in launching a satellite:

> Control of space means control of the world. From space the masters of infinity would have the power to control the earth's weather, to cause drought and flood, to change the tides and raise the levels of the sea, to divert the Gulf Stream and change temperate climates

to frigid. That is the ultimate position: the position of total control over earth that lies somewhere in outer space.[29]

Space-Based Systems

Some analysts called the 1991 Gulf War the first "space war" because military operations depended to such a large degree on space-

based systems. In addition to navigation, weather forecasting, and observation systems, the military utilized space-based platforms for communications, surveillance, and early missile-attack warnings.

Those systems were improved and all came into play during Operation Iraqi Freedom. Global positioning satellites that ring the globe allowed soldiers in the middle of featureless Iraqi deserts to know their exact location. Those same satellites, called Navstar, also helped guide the sophisticated JDAMs to their intended targets. Twenty-four Navstar satellites make up the GPS, orbiting roughly 12,500 miles above Earth. The GPS was developed by the U.S. military as a way to provide better coordinates and targeting information to troops. The GPS has now become ubiquitous in commercial applications as well and is increasingly installed in automobiles and is available in handheld devices to aid outdoorsmen. The GPS satellites orbit Earth once every twelve hours. They follow six orbital paths, with four satellites following each path. As the satellites make their way around Earth, they continually transmit a stream of coded radio signals that can be picked up by ground receivers. Signals from at least three satellites are needed to establish the location of any given position on Earth, so the orbits are synchronized in such a way that signals

A rocket lifts a global positioning satellite into space. Coalition forces used GPS systems to coordinate ground operations and to guide JDAMs.

from between five and eight of the satellites are available at all times at any point on the planet.

The GPS was updated during the Iraq War: On March 31, 2003, a new GPS satellite was launched into orbit to replace a satellite that had been part of the system for thirteen years, and another GPS satellite was replaced in July 2003.

The use of GPS technology was a huge asset in Operation Iraqi Freedom. The GPS signals are available twenty-four hours a day and thus allowed coalition forces to guide their JDAMs as well as determine their exact location and the precise positions of Iraqi troops at any time of day or night.

The Importance of Satellites

A variety of other satellites also aided the coalition by enhancing the ability of military planners to communicate with troops on the ground, see enemy positions, and detect emerging weather conditions. Approximately fifty satellites provided such diverse services as communications, surveillance, warnings, and weather forecasting to the Combined Forces Air Component commander. Weather forecasting was improved, and satellite imagery of Iraq allowed military planners to identify the locations of Iraqi troops and determine the best way to attack them. One satellite, the Advanced KH-11, is capable of detecting objects as small as four inches wide. Similar to the Hubble Space Telescope except for the fact that it points back at Earth instead of out into space, the KH-11 is capa-

Intelligence, Surveillance, and Reconnaissance

Utilizing technology that did not even exist at the time of Operation Desert Storm, military commanders in the 2003 war in Iraq were able to enjoy an unprecedented view of the battlefield. Through the use of drones—pilotless aircraft—coalition leaders always knew the precise locations of Iraqi troops and tanks, making them vulnerable to continued coalition assaults from both the air and the ground.

Coalition intelligence, surveillance, and reconnaissance craft, both manned and unmanned, flew one thousand missions during Operation Iraqi Freedom. They took forty-two thousand still images, thirty-two hundred hours of video, and another seventeen hundred hours of images of moving targets. Iraqi military commanders could not even communicate with each other without being overheard: Coalition electronic intelligence aircraft intercepted twenty-four hundred hours of Iraqi signals intelligence.

ble of shooting remarkably clear photos both day or night. Such images allowed planners to determine concentrations of Iraqi troops, movements of those troops, and other important information.

Satellites also played a large role in allowing for improved communications among troops, and efforts to improve the nation's system of military satellites continued during Operation Iraqi Freedom. For example, the military strategic, tactical, and relay system (MILSTAR) was enhanced on April 8, 2003, when the sixth MILSTAR satellite was launched into orbit, providing global coverage. MILSTAR is a network of satellites evenly spaced around the world in geosynchronous orbits. Originally envisioned as a way to conduct and win a nuclear war even if there were no survivors in the United States, MILSTAR provides the military with instantaneous global communications without the need for ground relays. MILSTAR allows for secure, jam-resistant communications between command centers, ships, subs, aircraft, and ground units.

JSTARS

Closer to Earth, air-based systems also contributed mightily to the coalition war effort in Iraq. For example, a joint army and air force program to provide better real-time information to soldiers on the ground resulted in the creation of the joint surveillance target attack radar system (JSTARS), an aircraft-based system that uses sophisticated radar sensors to track slow-moving vehicles at great distances. The sophisticated system is able to determine the direction, speed, and patterns of enemy ground vehicles and even helicopters. The planes can fly in friendly skies—its radar system has a range of 150 miles—while providing instant information to ground commanders about enemy battlefield movements. The ability to fly at a distance from the battlefield enhances the safety of the JSTARS crew of twenty-two, which includes three flight personnel and nineteen systems operators. For extended missions the craft carries a crew of thirty-four, with six flight personnel and twenty-eight systems operators.

The system is carried on an air force E-8C plane, essentially a modifed Boeing 707 that has been equipped with sophisticated radar, communications, operations, and control systems. One of the plane's most prominent external features is a forty-foot-long canoe-shaped radome, which is attached to the bottom of the plane and contains a twenty-four-foot-long, side-looking, phased-array antenna. By tilting the antenna to either side of the aircraft, this antenna can develop a 120-degree field of view covering 19,305 square miles. The radar system gathers detailed battlefield information, including detection of enemy helicopters, rotating antenna, and slow, low-flying enemy aircraft. JSTARS utilizes a powerful computer server to process and analyze the data. The four high-speed data processors on board are each capable of processing more than 600 million operations a second. This information is then relayed to army stations on the ground and to other command and control systems. The information is passed on to ground commanders through a variety of secure voice and datalinks. JSTARS has twelve encrypted UHF radios, two encrypted HF radios, three encrypted VHF radios, and other secure communications systems. A JSTARS plane can stay in the air for nine hours without refueling.

The JSTARS program was credited with providing improved information to ground forces during the Iraq War. According to air force lieutenant colonel Mick Quintrall, commander of the 363rd Expeditionary Airborne Command and Control Squadron, "Every Operation Iraqi Freedom ground commander has had a better understanding of the battlefield because of JSTARS contributions. . . . The JSTARS radar product to the battlefield commander and command and control centers has demonstrated improved moving ground target tracking and quicker sensor-to-commander nodes on the ground."[30]

Rivet Joint

Another significant information gathering plane is the RC-135V/2 Rivet Joint, a reconnaissance aircraft built on an extensively modified C-135 plane. Onboard sensors allow the plane's mission crew to detect, identify, and locate a wide range of electronic and communications signals em-

anating from the battlefield. Multiband receivers, antennae, and satellite data link equipment aboard the Rivet Joint search the battlefield for enemy radio, radar, satellite, and even cell phone transmissions and can pinpoint where those signals are coming from. The information gleaned by the Rivet Joint is forwarded to planners and commanders on the ground, who can then plan strikes against enemy communications and signalling positions. The Rivet Joint evolved from Cold War–era planes

The RC-35V/2 Rivet Joint reconnaissance aircraft can detect enemy communications signals and target the sources of transmission.

used by the Strategic Air Command for intelligence collection.

The Rivet Joint is operated by a flight crew that includes three pilots and two navigators and a mission crew that includes a minimum of twenty-one people—three electronic warfare officers, fourteen intelligence operators, and four maintenance technicians. The plane is powered by four turbofan engines that each provide more than sixteen thousand pounds of thrust. The Rivet Joint can fly at speeds in excess of five hundred miles per hour.

The plane is 135 feet long, 42 feet tall, and has a wingspan of 131 feet. The Rivet Joint can fly nearly four thousand miles before needing refueling.

Identifying Targets

The air and space surveillance assets utilized by the military helped to significantly streamline the process of identifying bombing and attack targets. In World War II, U.S. target planners could spend weeks planning a single strike against a fixed target that might involve hundreds of bombers. A combination of better information and more-precise weaponry has cut the planning process to a few hours and allows the targets to be struck with far fewer aircraft. Indeed, as Operation Iraqi Freedom unfolded, planners went from doing long-range preparations to planning contemporaneous attacks. "As the war progresses, we've done less and less deliberate [long-range] planning and more and more of the 'current ops' planning," said Captain Adam Gonzalez, chief of target de-

velopment with the Combined Air Operations Center's Intelligence, Surveillance, and Reconnaissance Targets Cell. "If Coalition forces positively identify a target during a morning mission, it'll likely be struck by sundown."[31]

Because the coalition was concerned about minimizing damage to Iraq's infrastructure, planners pored over satellite imagery and other data to find the best and yet least destructive means of beating the Iraqi military. At the beginning of the war, for example, analysts were concerned about the Iraqi air defense system. The system was highly sophisticated, with a command structure at its center and radar sites spread throughout the country. The system could have proved a serious threat to coalition aircraft, so members of Gonzalez's team looked for ways to put the system out of commission with greatest precision and least effort. The Intelligence, Surveillance, and Reconnaissance Targets Cell decided to hit weak spots in the system instead of attacking every site. The approach worked, the system collapsed, and coalition aircraft were able to fly over Iraq with near impunity.

Unmanned Aerial Vehicles

Although coalition pilots were relatively safe from enemy attack by air, there were still situations in which it would have been dangerous for pilots to fly. Making low reconnaissance flights to locate guerrilla fighters, for example, could expose pilots to danger from rocket launchers and other ground-to-air arms. One way around these dangers was to utilize pilotless aircraft, known more formally as unmanned aerial vehicles (UAVs).

As far back as 1917, the U.S. military has experimented with the use of UAVs. In 1935 the U.S. military developed its first reusable unmanned crafts. Continuous improvements brought greater use of the crafts between World War II and the Gulf War, and these relatively small planes were to see their share of action during Operation Iraqi Freedom as swarms of UAVs flew over Iraq during the active military phase of the war. Among other things, the pilotless craft offer advantages because they are relatively inexpensive and potentially help spare the lives of pilots, making them an invaluable addition to the coalition arsenal.

One UAV in the U.S. arsenal is the RQ/MQ-1A Predator, an unusual-looking twenty-seven-foot craft with a forty-eight-foot wingspan. The *R* in the name stands for "reconnaissance," while the *M* stands for "multi-role." The *Q* stands for "unmanned aircraft system," and the *1* designates that the craft is the first of a series of unmanned reconnaissance aircraft systems.

Predator Features

At its rear, two tail fins drop down to form an inverted V, above which a propeller helps to power the craft. The Predator has a 101-horsepower Rotax 914 four-cylinder engine, not unlike the engine found in an off-the-shelf snowmobile. The Predator cruises at about 84 miles per hour, but it can achieve a top speed of roughly 130 miles per hour.

The Cobra Ball

The RC-135 Cobra Ball aircraft played a unique role during Operation Iraqi Freedom. The flight crew, consisting of two pilots, two navigators, five electronic warfare officers, two in-flight maintenance technicians, and six mission specialists, was responsible for collecting both optical and electronic data on Iraqi ballistic missiles and reentry vehicles.

The Cobra Ball was just one of many specialized aircraft patrolling the skies over Iraq during the war collecting intelligence that both protected coalition forces and provided them with detailed information about the location of Iraqi troops. These eyes in the sky gave the coalition a nearly complete view of Iraq, allowing commanders to pursue Iraqi troops wherever they tried to move.

The Predator can operate at altitudes of up to twenty-five thousand feet.

A bulge in the front of the Predator's flat-bottomed fuselage holds the plane's satellite-dish antenna. The plane also contains electronic and optical sensors. A color television camera in the nose allows for remote navigation, and a daylight television camera, infrared imaging cameras, and a synthetic-aperture radar are used for reconnaissance.

The Predator is intended to be used as part of a system. A fully operational system is made up of four aircraft, a ground control station, a satellite link, and roughly eighty-two personnel to ensure continuous around-the-clock operations. The basic crew for each individual Predator is one pilot and two sensor operators.

The pilot flies the Predator at a console in the ground control station. By manipulating a joystick, the pilot can maneuver the craft while watching color images from the Predator's television nose camera. Predators aided in Operation Iraqi Freedom by providing surveillance of enemy troops and targeting information for attack aircraft. "We immediately pass on any data we gather to the people on the ground who need it," says Captain Traz Trzaskoma, a Predator pilot. "We've been watching for where the bad guys hide, move or want to hide. And if we're carrying Hellfire missiles, we can take care of a target ourselves."[32] The Predator can be outfitted with two laser-guided Hellfire antitank missiles, and armed Predators made key contributions in the Iraq War.

Unmanned Global Hawk aircraft helped coalition forces locate and eliminate Saddam Hussein's Republican Guard units.

Near the beginning of the war, for example, a Predator fired a Hellfire and destroyed an Iraqi mobile antiaircraft artillery gun outside Al Amarah in southern Iraq.

Information gleaned by Predators also helped a special forces team to avoid unnecessary danger. "A special forces team was going into an area, and at the last minute we [told them] their landing zone wasn't the best. We helped change the mission at the last second. Then we helped them find a better place to land,"[33] says Trzaskoma.

Global Hawk

Another UAV making a significant contribution to the coalition war effort was the Global Hawk, a larger vehicle than the Predator. The Global Hawk has a wingspan of 116 feet, longer than that of the large Boeing 737 airliner. The Global Hawk has a jet engine and can fly close to 400 miles per hour at altitudes of up to 65,000 feet. The Global Hawk has extremely long range: It is capable of flying 13,500 nautical miles and operating up to thirty-six hours at a time.

Just as in the smaller Predator, the Global Hawk has a bulging nose that contains a satellite dish. In addition, the plane is packed with high-tech surveillance equipment such as a synthetic-aperture radar and high-resolution electro-optical and infrared sensors. These high-resolution sensors are capable of providing clear images through all sorts of weather. The Global Hawk can provide complete surveillance over an area the size of Illinois in just twenty-four hours.

Unlike the Predator, the Global Hawk is not piloted by a soldier at a remote location. Instead, the Global Hawk is fed a mission plan into its onboard computer system prior to takeoff. The computer checks to make sure all systems are operating correctly prior to takeoff. The Global Hawk has four global positioning systems on board to keep it on track. Soldiers do take an active role in the Global Hawk's operation, however. Monitoring the plane at ground stations, they point the plane's sensors in order to get the best quality images, which are then sent by satellite to field commanders. Moreover,

Demoralizing the Enemy

Civil War general William Tecumseh Sherman is often credited with being the father of modern warfare. Combining both military strength and psychological operations, Sherman led his Union troops on a rampage through the heart of the South.

Sherman's fabled "March to the Sea" brought widespread destruction to farms, railroads, and factories in the Confederacy. The destructive march had the effect of demoralizing civilians, who withdrew their active support of the Confederate war effort, and reduced the will of Confederate soldiers to fight as they worried about their families back home.

Today, military planners often use the threat of massive destruction as a means of demoralizing the enemy. For example, the U.S. Air Force's public demonstration of its powerful massive ordnance air-blast bomb carried an implied threat of destruction to Iraqi troops and was intended to reduce their will to fight.

Global Hawk operators can change the plane's mission as needs warrant simply by sending signals from the ground to the craft.

Military leaders credited the Global Hawk with helping to crush the Iraqi Republican Guard, Hussein's best fighters and most loyal troops. The Global Hawk flew surveillance missions over Baghdad, collecting some thirty-seven hundred images. Although the Global Hawk flew only 5 percent of surveillance missions during Operation Iraqi Freedom, it accounted for more than 55 percent of information on time-sensitive targets. Lieutenant Colonel Guy Cooper of the Twelfth Reconnaissance Squadron stationed at Beale Air Force Base in California, says the Global Hawk helped shorten the war.

Despite the sophisticated technology at its disposal, planners sometimes got their best information from forces on the ground. During Operation Iraqi Freedom, coalition commanders made extensive use of special operations forces for a host of activities, in-cluding reconnaissance and surveillance. Indeed, special operations forces infiltrated Iraq prior to the formal start of the war, identifying militarily significant targets that were subsequently bombed when the war began. Fanning out across Iraq, often traveling in pickup trucks, special operations forces continued to roam the country once the war began as part of ongoing surveillance and reconnaissance missions. The intelligence gleaned from such activities allowed the coalition to select bombing targets and attack tactics.

From planes and munitions to surveillance, the U.S.-led coalition enjoyed unquestioned technological superiority over Iraqi forces loyal to Saddam Hussein. However, the military also worked to erode loyalty to Hussein through a series of extensive psychological operations activities. These efforts were aimed not at killing Iraqi soldiers but at defeating them psychologically so that they would surrender rather than fight.

Chapter 7

Psychological Operations: "Your Cause Is Lost"

Psychological operations have become an integral part of modern warfare. Aimed at reducing an enemy's will to fight and sowing doubt in the enemy's mind about the battlefield prospects, psychological operations generally are focused on both military and civilian populations in a bid to undermine an opposition nation's resolve. As it has in previous wars, the U.S. military made full use of psychological operations before, during, and after the Iraq War as part of its strategy to oust Saddam Hussein from power and establish a democratic government in Iraq.

Radio Broadcasts

Military commanders have used radio as a primary medium in psychological operations since World War II. During the 1991 Gulf War, the United States used a small number of EC-130 Commando Solo aircraft to broadcast propaganda to Iraqi troops. Calling itself "the Voice of the Gulf," the psychological operations mission used a mix of popular

music and pointed messages that spoke to the futility of resisting the coming coalition assault. As a result, an estimated eighty-seven thousand Iraqi troops surrendered.

Retired U.S. general Wesley K. Clark, who served as a media analyst during the Iraq War, says the United States utilized similar tactics in Operation Iraqi Freedom. Among other things, the military tried to

impede Iraqi preparations through misinformation, deception, and psychological operations using the news media, journalists, former Iraqi generals, and direct communications, including e-mail with Iraqi leaders. The intent was to persuade Iraqis to lay down their arms, to refrain from using chemical and biological weapons even if ordered to do so, and to defect. This was the so-called information war. It had become a major growth industry inside the military since the 1991 war in the Gulf; it promised success more cheaply, with fewer casualties, by using modern technology and exploiting so-called asymmetric U.S. advantages.[34]

Picking up where the Voice of the Gulf left off following the Gulf War, the military launched what it called Information Radio in December 2002 as Pentagon officials began to prepare for war in Iraq. To make sure Iraqis knew about the broadcasts, coalition aircraft dropped hundreds of thousands of leaflets. And to be certain that Iraqis could hear the broadcasts, coalition special forces and intelligence agents covertly entered the country and distributed a large number of both solar-powered and hand-crank shortwave radios along with instructions on how to tune into Arabic-language broadcasts that urged cooperation with coalition troops. At the outset, Information Radio was directed primarily at Iraqi troops and government officials. The messages urged the Iraqis to lay down their arms.

Expanding the Audience

By March 2003, however, the broadcasts were aimed at Iraqi civilians as well. Air-dropped leaflets urged ordinary Iraqis to listen to the broadcasts for "important news and information. Coalition Forces Support the Iraqi people in their desire to remove Saddam and his Regime. The Coalition wishes no harm to the innocent Iraqi civilians."[35] When coalition bombs began to fall on Baghdad at the start of the Iraq War, an EC-130 Commando Solo plane jammed Iraqi state radio and replaced it with a pro-coalition broadcast. Among other things, listeners could hear a speaker in Arabic say, "This is the day we have been waiting for. The attack on Iraq has begun."[36] At all times, the broadcasts attempted to drive a wedge between the Iraqi people and Hussein. In one broadcast, Iraqis were told that

> Saddam has built palace after palace for himself and has purchased a fleet of luxury cars all at the expense of the Iraqi people. This money would be much better suited to build libraries and schools. This money would have gone a long way to provide better food and medicine for the people of Iraq. The amount of money Saddam spends on himself in one day would be more than enough to feed a family for a year.[37]

Another message directed to the Iraqi public attempted to get Iraqi civilians to withdraw their support for the Iraqi military. In it, Iraqis were told, "Do not let Saddam tarnish the reputation of soldiers any longer. Saddam uses the military to persecute those who don't agree with his unjust agenda. Make the decision."[38]

The U.S. Central Intelligence Agency also helped to fund and operate other radio stations in an attempt to build a rift between the citizenry and Hussein. One such station was the so-called Radio Tikrit, named after Hussein's birthplace. Radio Tikrit routinely criticized Hussein's leadership.

Coalition forces brought home the same message using cruder, low-technology

A Commando Solo plane receives fuel in flight. The EC-130 was used to broadcast procoalition messages over Iraqi radio.

methods after the shooting war started. Trucks outfitted with bullhorns roamed the streets of Iraqi cities, announcing in Arabic that the coalition forces were in Iraq to liberate the country from Saddam Hussein's despotic rule. In the village of Kifl, an armored Humvee slowly traveled through the streets, warning civilians to stay indoors and ordering Iraqi soldiers to give up the fight. "Your cause is lost,"[39] the soldiers were told in Arabic. However, the bullhorn campaigns were met with mixed success. Lieutenant Colonel Jeffrey Randall Sanderson, commander of the armored division that rolled into Kifl, noted, "He's broadcasting, 'Surrender, surrender, surrender,' and they ain't surrendering. I don't know why not. If they want to fight it out, we'll fight it out."[40]

Using the Internet

In addition to using the airwaves to spread propaganda in its information-warfare campaign, the United States also attempted to bring its propaganda techniques into the computer age. The military, for example, used the Internet in an attempt to persuade Iraqi leaders not to use weapons of mass destruction against U.S. and coalition forces. In January 2003 the U.S. Department of Defense began to send thousands of e-mail messages to Iraqi military leaders promising protection to those who agreed not to use such weapons. Analysts commenting on the e-mail program said that the most difficult element in conducting such an operation would be in finding accurate e-mail addresses. However, once that was accomplished, it would be relatively easy to send repeated messages to the officials. The campaign marked the first time the military had ever used e-mail as part of its information-warfare program.

The e-mail messages contained the subject line "Important Information," and read:

- If you provide information on weapons of mass destruction or you take steps to hamper their use, we will do what is necessary to protect you and protect your families. Failing to do that will lead to grave personal consequences.

- If you took part in the use of these ugly weapons, you'll be regarded as war criminals.
- If you can make these weapons ineffective, then do it. If you can identify the position of weapons of mass destruction by light signals, then do it.
- If all this is not possible, then at least refuse to take part in any activity or follow orders to use weapons of mass destruction.[41]

The e-mail messages also stated that Iraq's programs to build chemical, biological, and

A U.S. soldier guards satellite equipment in Tikrit. The coalition used the media to help turn the Iraqi people against Saddam Hussein.

nuclear weapons violated that country's international treaties and obligations to the United Nations. The messages noted that, as a result, Iraq had become isolated internationally.

The e-mail barrage continued after the war started. At a press conference on March 20, 2003 Defense Secretary Donald Rumsfeld confirmed that the Defense Department was "in communication with still more people who are officials of the [Iraqi] military at various levels."[42] The messages again warned against the use of weapons of mass destruction and also urged the officials not to take up conventional arms against the coalition forces. Moreover, the messages said the coalition effort was one to liberate Iraq from Saddam Hussein, not to conquer or subjugate the country.

Another unique aspect of the coalition's psychological operations program included phone calls to Iraqi military officials from U.S. psychological operations specialists. The phone calls stressed the same points as the e-mail messages. In addition to emphasizing the severity of consequences for resisting the coalition or using weapons of mass destruction, the e-mail and phone calls also had the unnerving effect of making the Iraqi officials feel as though they could not hide from U.S. forces.

Surrender and Disobedience Is Urged

The so-called information war was not confined to military leaders. Indeed, many messages were aimed at lower-level troops, the

Television

Radio broadcasts and leaflet drops are traditional means of spreading propaganda during wartime. Coalition forces used both in an attempt to drive a wedge between Iraqi citizens and Saddam Hussein as well as to reduce the willingness of Iraqi troops to fight.

Once coalition forces had taken control of Baghdad, however, they decided to add television broadcasts to their information-warfare campaign. On April 10, 2003, the day after Baghdad was seized, coalition forces established Towards Freedom TV. The new station utilized Iraqi journalists but carried a decidedly pro-coalition slant. The first program, for example, carried an interview with a leader of a group hostile to Hussein and reports on humanitarian aid provided by coalition troops.

fighting men who made up Iraq's military. U.S. psychological operations forces dropped millions of leaflets before and during the war urging Iraqi soldiers to lay down their arms and surrender or face certain annihilation. A leaflet dropped over southern Iraq on October 28, 2002, for example, pictured an Iraqi soldier and an antiaircraft gun. In Arabic, the text read, "Before you engage Coalition aircraft, think about the consequences." On the back, an Iraqi soldier was pictured surrounded by smoke and shrapnel from an exploded coalition bomb, while an Iraqi mother holding two children was pictured off to the side. The text on that side of the leaflet read, "Think about your family. Do what you must to survive."[43]

The leaflets' messages became increasingly sophisticated and specific. On

November 28, 2003, for example, coalition aircraft dropped 360,000 leaflets near a military communications site that had been bombed a week earlier. The leaflets warned against repairing military fiber-optic cables, saying that they had been targeted for obliteration. The leaflets warned that anyone working to repair the cables was at risk of perishing during coalition bombing runs.

Other leaflets urged Iraqi citizens to stay away from areas occupied by Iraqi troops. The leaflets stated that, though the coalition did not want to injure citizens, they could be endangering their lives by being in close proximity to Iraqi soldiers. Among other things, these leaflets pictured Iraqi weapons stashed near schools and mosques.

As the war neared, leaflet drops were increasingly focused on Iraqi troops themselves. Some urged them to walk away from their weapons and surrender. Others urged troops simply to quit the military by going absent without leave. One such leaflet had a photo of a dead Iraqi soldier in the center with the text, "Do not risk your life— and the lives of your comrades." On the back of that leaflet, a child was pictured in school on the left half, and a family portrait was on the right. The text stated, "Leave now and go home—Watch your children learn, grow and prosper."[44] Still other leaflets spelled out precisely how Iraqi troops could avoid being killed by coalition forces. Iraqis were instructed to park their military vehicles in squares, display a white flag on all vehicles, and gather in groups away from the vehicles. The leaflets stated that, although officers could retain their sidearms, all other troops were required to leave their weapons behind.

Leaflets also stressed the importance of oil to the nation's postwar recovery. In some leaflets, Iraqis were warned not to release oil into the environment, a step coalition officials feared Hussein might order. The leaflets warned that dumping oil would pollute Iraq's waters and diminish the country's chance for an economic recovery. Another series of leaflets showed a burning oil refinery. The text warned that destroying the nation's oil industry would ruin the country's livelihood.

Language as a Weapon

The coalition used almost every possible means to influence Iraqis to avoid resisting the coalition's military advance. The very terminology employed by U.S. military planners was intended to instill fear in Iraqi soldiers. In one of the most ubiquitous phrases of the war, military commanders promised a campaign that would inspire both shock and awe. The military's buildup to war reinforced the message. The U.S. Navy provided a show of military might intended to rattle the Iraqi military leadership psychologically. Five carrier strike groups, three amphibious-ready groups, and two amphibious task forces totaling more than 200 coalition ships, 81,000 sailors, and 15,500 U.S. Marines were positioned in the Persian Gulf and the Mediterranean Sea prior to March 2003,

A Brave New World

During World War II it often took planners weeks to map out an air campaign to take out a single structure, such as a factory. The campaign would have required the use of hundreds of bombers dropping so-called dumb bombs in order to have any hope for success.

During Operation Iraqi Freedom, lead time for strategic strikes was drastically reduced. In the space of one hour, for example, intelligence agents learned that Saddam Hussein and his sons would be meeting in a bunker in a Baghdad neighborhood. Four special forces operators working in Baghdad independently learned about the meeting and quickly forwarded the information to commanders. Commanders sent the information to an air force airborne command-and-control aircraft,

which then summoned a B-1 bomber loaded with bunker-busting munitions. The B-1 dropped four two-thousand-pound precision-guided bombs on the structure, flattening it. From intelligence to bombing, the operation was stunning in its speed.

Hussein, it was learned, was not in the building when the bombs were dropped. Nevertheless, the operation demonstrated that modern military commanders were now able to order almost instantaneous strategic strikes with a single plane to accomplish what used to take weeks and hundreds of bombers.

A munitions technician loads bunker-buster bombs onto aircraft. Precision weapons made traditional carpet bombing unnecessary.

Iraqi information minister Mohammed Saeed al-Sahaf tried to deceive the Iraqi people into believing that Iraq was winning the war.

ready to enter the conflict when needed. Once the war began, the ships launched Tomahawk missiles and carrier-based fighter-bomber jets, providing the U.S. and coalition military effort with enormous firepower. The effort was the largest ever concentration of naval firepower and technology in so small a geographic area.

The coalition made good on its prewar threats with extensive precision bombing of facilities useful to the Iraqi military machine and coupled that with a headlong rush by ground troops toward Baghdad. The offensive was geared toward making the Iraqi government—and Iraqi citizens—believe that there was no way the United States and coalition partners would lose.

U.S. military leaders also openly spoke of new weapons that could wreak widespread havoc throughout Iraq. For example, they discussed a new weapon that allegedly could flash millions of watts of electricity, causing a surge that would shut down computers and create blackouts throughout Iraq. Another new weapon was tested in a very public way by the U.S. Air Force on March 11, 2003. The weapon was the 21,700-pound super bomb called the massive ordnance air-blast bomb (MOAB). As the bomb is guided by satellite to its intended target, it releases fuel that is then ignited, creating an enormous explosion. The public test of the bomb was an attempt to intimidate the Iraqi leadership and military. A MOAB was then publicly delivered to the Iraqi theater in another attempt to intimidate the Iraqis.

At the same time, however, the U.S. military made much of the fact that it was relying extensively on precision bombs in its air-war campaign. The use of such weapons, which reduced the number and likelihood of civilian casualties, was carefully calibrated to both increase the effectiveness of coalition efforts and sway Iraqis into believing that the coalition wanted only to remove Saddam Hussein from power, not wage a war of occupation against the Iraqi people. In addition, the coalition attempted to minimize damage to Iraq's infrastructure to help expedite the nation's rebuilding after the war as well as to minimize disruptions to civilians.

Media Access

Even the way the war was covered by news organizations was part of the U.S. psychological operations offensive. Unlike the Gulf War, when reporters were kept well away from the fighting, the military in the Iraq War decided to allow reporters to travel with military combat units. Called embedding, reporters lived and traveled with troops. Wesley Clark said the plan was a stroke of genius because it allowed journalists "to show the human face of the U.S. forces, along with unprecedented real-time

---

Leaflet Campaigns

Coalition aircraft dropped millions of leaflets on Iraq before, during, and after the military phase of the Iraq War. The leaflets each carried a targeted message designed either to reassure Iraqi civilians about the coalition's intentions or to warn Iraqi troops not to resist the coalition assault.

Hundreds of different leaflets were developed and designed during Operation Iraqi Freedom, but not all were used. One leaflet warned owners of ships that their craft would be confiscated if they helped Iraqi leaders flee the country. Though this leaflet was not dropped, copies began to circulate in Bahrain.

Other leaflets were designed to demoralize Iraqi troops. One, for example, pictured U.S. fighter-bombers. The leaflet, in Arabic, warned that coalition aircraft could hit any spot in Iraq at any time of day or night. The leaflet also warned against attacking the aircraft, an act that would bring instant and deadly retaliation.

---

access to the uncertainties, fears, and hardships of the ground battle. It was . . . a program that won great sympathy for the American forces in the field."[45] The worldwide coverage of the U.S.-led offensive also had the effect of alarming Iraqi officials. Though they gamely tried to insist that the coalition forces had been stalled by heroic Iraqi defenses, images on the television screens of Iraqi citizens clearly showed otherwise. In a bid to limit the damage, the government of Iraq kicked the CNN news crew out of the country.

Iraq, of course, also attempted to wage an offensive psychological-warfare campaign of its own. The Iraqi information minister, Mohammed Saeed al-Sahaf, routinely gave press briefings claiming great Iraqi battle successes that were illusory. Even when U.S. troops had infiltrated Baghdad, al-Sahaf was claiming that the coalition forces had been repelled. "There are no American infidels in Baghdad,"[46] al-Sahaf said. So wildly false were al-Sahaf's claims throughout the war that U.S. soldiers ridiculed him with derived nicknames such as "Comical Ali" and "Baghdad Bob." Oliver North, who was embedded with a U.S. Marine unit for Fox News, recalled how al-Sahaf claimed that no U.S. troops were near Baghdad and that U.S. forces had been run off from Saddam International Airport in Baghdad. "Ironically, just as FOX News Channel is showing him telling the Iraqis that the Americans were nowhere near Baghdad, they also put up a split screen showing U.S. Army tanks parked on the lawn of one of Saddam's palaces."[47]

Iraqi officials, of course, also attempted to wage a war for hearts and minds around the world. They used whatever material was at hand in an attempt to sway public opinion, both domestically and internationally. For example, when an explosion rocked a busy Baghdad market, Iraqi government officials were quick to blame the resulting deaths of Iraqi citizens on an American bomb. The United States said the explosion had most likely been caused by an Iraqi missile. However, images of dead Iraqis temporarily dominated news coverage worldwide and helped inflame anti-American passions in Europe.

The United States and its coalition partners made a concerted effort during the Iraq War to convince Iraqis that it was futile to fight. With a host of persuasive tools, ranging from raw demonstrations of military might to massive leaflet drops, the U.S. military engaged in widespread and sustained psychological operations. These operations were geared toward easing the fears of ordinary Iraqi citizens while at the same time convincing Iraq's soldiers to surrender. Psychological operations, coupled with the coalition's enormous technological superiority over Iraq, provided the U.S.-led forces with a major advantage in the war. However, the coalition nevertheless faced serious difficulties during Operation Iraqi Freedom and found that technology alone was not a guarantee of military success.

The Limits of Technological Superiority

The vast superiority of the technology utilized by coalition forces against the Iraqi military made Operation Iraqi Freedom seem in many ways to be a one-sided conflict. The U.S. military was able to see its enemy at great distances, target it, and bomb it accurately in all weather conditions. However, not everything ran smoothly for the coalition during the war, and the harsh desert conditions of Iraq exposed serious shortcomings in the coalition attack. Moreover, sophisticated weaponry by itself was ineffective against so-called asymmetric attacks—ambushes by guerrilla soldiers, attacks by soldiers dressed as civilians, car-bomb attacks, and fake surrenders that presaged an ongoing insurgency movement.

The general effectiveness of the coalition attack is hard to dispute. In roughly a month, the military was able to defeat a four-hundred-thousand-man military, topple a ruthless dictator, and successfully engage in urban combat operations while suffering fewer than two hundred combat deaths. Utilizing assets ranging from space-based communications and reconnaissance satellites to laser-guided missiles and overwhelming firepower, the coalition enjoyed extraordinarily swift military success.

Failed Decapitation Strikes

Nevertheless, the military was to learn that merely having a technological advantage was sometimes not enough to bring quick victory. For example, on roughly fifty occasions during Operation Iraqi Freedom planners unleashed a torrent of smart weapons on sites suspected of harboring Saddam Hussein and other top Iraqi figures, so-called decapitation strikes designed to bring the Iraqi resistance to a quick end. The weapons themselves operated as expected, delivering massive destructive power with pinpoint accuracy. However, no Iraqi leaders were killed in the strikes, which instead claimed the lives of dozens of Iraqi civilians.

In one attempt on the life of Hussein and his sons, Qusay and Uday, B-1 bombers dropped four so-called bunker-buster bombs on a building in the civilian quarter of Baghdad in an attack that ultimately claimed the lives of some fourteen people. The Husseins, however, were not among them.

The decapitation strikes were ordered based on intelligence that the Iraqi leaders were at a specified location, which had been identified by telephone-call intercepts. Because Iraqi leaders used Thuraya satellite phones, which contain a global positioning system (GPS) chip, intelligence officials were confident that once they intercepted a call, they could determine the location of the caller. However, lag times between the intercept and getting a bomber to the area were apparently long enough to allow the leaders to escape. In one case, for example, a bomber arrived at a target within forty-five minutes of the call intercept—an amazingly rapid response—but not in time to kill the caller, who had moved from the area. Moreover, the Thuraya GPS chip is only accurate to within a radius of one hundred meters; even if the leaders had remained at the spot in which they placed their calls, they could still be a good football field away from where the smart bombs were dropped.

On April 8, 2003, B-1 bombers were used in a decapitation strike that resulted in the deaths of fourteen civilians.

The Imperfect Art of Intelligence

The coalition's rapidly stunning victory in the Iraq War was a model of military efficiency. Seamlessly weaving the combined attack force of the U.S. Navy, Army, Marine Corps, and Air Force, as well as military forces from several other countries, coalition commanders demonstrated a new breed of warfare that allowed a rapid victory with far fewer forces than would have been deemed possible even ten years previous.

But although the military enjoyed dramatic success, the U.S. intelligence community drew poor reviews. The war itself had been predicated on intelligence that Saddam Hussein had stockpiled weapons of mass destruction and had intentions of sharing these weapons with terrorist groups.

Nearly a year after the war had been waged and won, teams of experts scouring Iraq had been unable to locate any of the weapons that intelligence reports indicated were in Iraq in abundance.

Commenting on the failure to find weapons of mass destruction in Iraq, air force general Richard B. Myers, chairman of the Joint Chiefs of Staff, said on February 10, 2004, that intelligence gathering was far from a science. As related in a press release found at the Department of Defense Web site, Myers said that intelligence agencies "have had great success, and they have sometimes missed the mark; that's the nature of their business. You will never make the baseball all-star team in the intelligence business."

Similarly, smart weapons are only as effective as the information given them. The Iranian government complained, for example, that some coalition munitions had actually landed in Iranian territory. These bombs apparently had been incorrectly programmed, with potentially disastrous effects.

No Prohibited Weapons Found

The limits of technology were evident as well in the issue of Iraq's weapons of mass destruction, weapons that theoretically could be used by terrorists to strike at the United States and its friends in the Middle East and around the globe. Their existence was the primary reason given by the Bush administration for the Iraq War. Detailed, top-secret satellite images of various sites in Iraq were produced in an attempt to build international support for the impending war. In ad-

dition, government officials provided other intelligence based on interviews with Iraqis who allegedly had information about a secret weapons program within Iraq. However, despite devoting significant resources to the task, the military was unable to find any evidence of such weapons, even though it had free rein in Iraq following war's end.

Weather Problems

The natural environment likewise showed that technology has limits. Sandstorms in particular slowed the coalition ground offensive. Called *shamals*, the sandstorms severely limited visibility, sometimes blocking out the sun. On March 25, for example, the sixth day of the war, powerful sandstorms blackened the skies over central Iraq, greatly slowing the advance of ground troops who previously had been closing in with great speed on Baghdad from the south and west. During the height of the sandstorms, troops were forced to hunker down and wait for the storms to dissipate before continuing on toward Baghdad.

The foul weather made it extremely difficult for land vehicles and helicopters to operate, and it made the lives of ground troops miserable as sand pelted their exposed skin. However, bombers operating at great altitudes were still able—with the aid of joint directional attack munitions—to make pinpoint strikes against Republican Guard positions around Baghdad, making the eventual advance of the ground troops somewhat safer. Nevertheless, sandstorms became such an issue for coalition forces that the Naval Research Laboratory in Monterey, California, developed a model to produce three-day dust forecasts during Operation Iraqi Freedom. But merely knowing when the sandstorms would be troublesome did nothing to stop them. Moreover, all the technology at the disposal of the military was powerless to help the ground troops advance when the storms were at their worst. And not only the troops themselves were stalled. The ferocious sandstorms sometimes delayed the delivery of needed supplies to forward ground troop positions, supplies that included both food and ammunition.

Low-tech, not high-tech, solutions proved the most effective weapons against microscopic parasites that took a toll on coalition forces. Bites from sand flies infected with cutaneous leishmaniasis led to widespread infection among troops. Infection by the parasite causes weeping sores that can take up to a year to heal. Sand flies are most active in Iraq on warm nights from March to October, meaning troops bitten at the beginning of the conflict stood a good chance of becoming infected. It was not until the beginning of the war that officials recognized the problem, which could be avoided by simply using insect repellant containing DEET, applying an insecticide on clothing, and sleeping under mosquito netting treated with insecticide. However, as coalition forces made their lightning trek through Iraq at the beginning of the war, they often slept wherever they could, not realizing the danger the sand flies presented. An estimated five hundred soldiers were treated for infection by the parasite.

Poorly Supplied Troops

The U.S. technological advantage also was thwarted at times because of a lack of adequate resources. One of the signal achievements of the military has been the development of the global positioning system, which, in addition to guiding smart bombs with great precision, theoretically allows troops to know exactly where they are at any given time. However, shortages in the military version of the GPS receivers meant that many of the soldiers in Operation Iraqi Freedom went into battle either without any GPS receivers or with less precise, commercially available GPS receivers. This shortfall meant that soldiers could lose their bearings in the monotonous featurelessness of the harsh Iraqi desert.

Sandstorms routinely slowed coalition ground forces as they advanced on Baghdad.

Reports also indicate a lack of standard uniforms and protective gear. For example, although the military continued to hail the benefits of the armor given to troops, some reservists complained they had been given substandard equipment. A U.S. National Guard trooper at home in New Jersey on a rest-and-relaxation trip went on a local radio show to complain that he and other guardsmen had been sent to Iraq with shoddy body armor. Joseph Fabozzi complained that many guardsmen had been issued older body armor vests that, while capable of stopping a knife, were no match for rounds from an AK-47 rifle, the standard weapon of the Iraqi soldier. Fabozzi claimed that many of his colleagues had in desper-

ation turned to confiscated Iraqi armor vests, which were superior to the vests issued to members of the National Guard.

Such shortages were reported most often among reservists. Members of the Eighty-first Infantry Brigade of the Washington Army National Guard scrambled to find desert boots and other items such as flashlights and binoculars because the unit had not been adequately supplied. Some reservists chose to purchase these much-needed supplies rather than wait for the army to supply them. Desert combat boots, for example, were hard to get through normal supply channels. "There were a lot of reports . . . that prior to the war, people would go out and buy their own gear," according to Patrick Garrett, an analyst with GlobalSecurity.Org. "The army ran out of desert camo boots, and a lot of soldiers were being issued regular black combat boots. Soldiers decided that wasn't for them, so they paid for new boots with their own money."[48]

In a preliminary study analyzing lessons learned in the Iraq War, the Pentagon found that soldiers spent their own money to purchase better field radios, extra ammunition carriers, and commercial backpacks. In addition, some soldiers bought their own night-vision goggles, satellite-based positioning systems, and shortwave radios.

The Rapid Ground Offensive Creates Problems

Another advantage for the coalition force was its vast communications network, augmented with satellite links in addition to standard over-the-air communications. However, the rapid advance of the coalition ground offensive highlighted flaws in the communications system. Units that straggled because their heavy vehicles foundered in the soft sands of the Iraqi desert or simply broke down in the harsh desert terrain found themselves cut off from other troops, who quickly outdistanced them. Many soldiers found that their military-issue radios did not perform well, and they relied instead on off-the-shelf Motorolas they purchased themselves, which they maintained had better range and reliability.

Supply Problems

The coalition's ground offensive was stunning: Ground troops swarmed into Iraq from Kuwait and advanced toward Baghdad in one of the most rapid advances in the history of warfare. The speed of operations, however, created problems for some troops because supply convoys were unable to keep pace with the advancing fighting units. Colonel David C. Hackworth, an outspoken critic of U.S. military planning for the Iraq War, reported receiving hundreds of complaints from soldiers on the front lines in a Jonathan Franklin article on the Common Dreams News Center Web site on August 5, 2003: "Soldiers get literally hundreds of flea or mosquito bites and they can't get cream or Benadryl to keep the damn things from itching." "We did not receive a single piece of parts support for our vehicles during the entire battle. . . . Not a single repair part has made [it] to our vehicles to date. . . . My unit had abandoned around 12 vehicles."

Hackworth continues:

One letter I got today, written by a sergeant in a tank unit, said that of its 18 armored vehicles—Bradley or Abrams—only four are operational. The rest were down because of burned-out transmissions or the tracks eaten out. So it is not just the [bad] food and bad water—a soldier can live with short rations—but spare parts, baby! If you don't have them, your weapons don't work. Most of the resupply is by wheeled vehicles, and the roads and terrain out there is gobbling up tires like you won't believe. Michelin's whole production for civilians has been stopped [at certain plants] and have dedicated their entire production to the U.S. military in Iraq—and they can't keep up!

The remarkable and rapid advance of the ground offensive also had another unintended consequence. Coalition forces barrelled into Iraq from Kuwait and ate up an enormous amount of ground in a relatively short amount of time. However, the result was that soldiers became extremely fatigued, impairing judgment and making even routine actions subject to error. Such errors proved especially costly when the troops encountered determined resistance from Iraqi soldiers.

Equipment Malfunction

Ground troops also contended with jammed weapons. Many reported that their carbines jammed on firing, obviously a serious malfunction. A postwar military analysis found that the culprit was a faulty gun lubricant known as CLP that was found to be ineffective in preventing sand and dirt from building up on weapons.

Widely issued to troops, CLP was already suspect in the eyes of some commanders, who turned to a more effective lubricant, called MILITEC-1 Synthetic Metal Conditioner. Troops that did not receive MILITEC-1, however, quickly learned that CLP, instead of repelling dirt and sand, appeared to instead attract it to their weapons.

Other soldiers had the exact opposite problem with their M4s. Many found that the weapons could be fired even when set to the "safe" position, a dangerous scenario when troops were surrounded by fellow soldiers or friendly Iraqi citizens. Still other soldiers were generally satisfied with the performance of the M4 but complained that the weapons lost effectiveness at longer ranges.

The 507th Maintenance Company

A case study in the limits of technology is the now-famous story of the army's 507th Maintenance Company, which through an avoidable navigation error found itself in an ambush in Nasiriyah. The 507th found itself last in a convoy of six hundred vehicles and lost communication with the main body of the convoy when it was forced to stop to recover heavy vehicles stuck in the sand and provide assistance as vehicles broke down. In Nasiriyah, the 507th was supposed to head north to support a Patriot antimissile battery. Instead, the group took a wrong turn and ended up in a section of town controlled by Iraqi paramilitary forces and regular soldiers.

Traveling in Humvees, members of the 507th quickly became aware of another problem that was to plague coalition forces during the war and in the later peacekeeping role troops were to play: Most of the Humvees sent to Iraq were not armored, and they proved vulnerable to attacks from rocket-propelled grenades, mines, and even fire from the AK-47 rifles utilized by Iraqi troops. Such was the case with the Humvees used by the 507th, which were quickly disabled by rocket-propelled grenades. The driver of one Humvee, Private First Class Lori Ann Piestewa, lost control of the vehicle, which crashed. Piestewa later died of injuries sustained in the crash. Private First

Class Jessica Lynch was injured in the crash and taken prisoner. First Sergeant Robert Dowdy attempted to reorganize the thirteen-vehicle convoy into a safe retreat, but his Humvee was hit by a grenade and he was killed. Other members of the 507th attempted to fight their way out of the ambush, but they were forced to surrender when their guns jammed.

Vehicle Vulnerability

The problem of unarmored Humvees quickly became a major issue for the military, which was generally satisfied with the Humvee's performance as a multipurpose vehicle; Humvees can, among other things, be configured as troop and cargo carriers,

missile carriers, ambulances, and scout vehicles. Most Humvees, however, have canvas roofs and doors, certainly no match for enemy munitions. Just a little over two hundred armored Humvees were sent to Iraq at the beginning of the war, and once operations started, the Pentagon placed increasing orders for more. However, retrofitting Humvees with armor is a time-consuming process, and the effort reduces the passenger- and cargo-carrying capacity of the hulking vehicles. When armored, the Humvee can seat just three passengers despite its enor-

Although Humvees were extremely mobile in the Iraqi deserts, the unarmored vehicles offered little protection against enemy fire.

Sometimes Failures Were Successes

On April 1, 2003 a U.S. Navy pilot and crewman were forced to bail out of an F-14 Tomcat fighter jet over Iraq because of a mechanical failure on the plane. The men were able to parachute safely to the ground, but they were trapped in Iraqi-controlled territory.

The Sixty-sixth Rescue Squadron, utilizing Pave Hawk helicopters, were able to rescue the two men. Major Bob Walker of the Sixty-sixth reported that the men were safely rescued but that they had been in danger. The Sixty-sixth's Pave Hawks participated in a number of rescues during the war; although the helicopters and their crews did not take direct fire, tracer fire was observed on several missions.

The Pave Hawk is a modifed version of the army Black Hawk helicopter. It is designed to operate day or night in hostile enemy skies to recover downed airmen or trapped soldiers.

mous size. The armor process involves adding ballistic plastic windows and armor reinforcement to allow the vehicle to sustain hits from assault rifles, overhead bursts from cannons, and mine blasts.

In the meantime, soldiers attempted to fashion their own Humvee protection. Captain Darryl M. Butler, an engineer with the Task Force First Armored Division, put together a field kit to increase the protection afforded in an unarmored Humvee. Butler became a minor celebrity in the war, and his invention became known as the "Butler mobile." Other soldiers filled their Humvees with sandbags to gain added protection, but the weight of the bags had a tendency to take away from the vehicle's overall stability. To protect themselves from mines, unarmored Humvees sometimes traveled single file behind a lead Humvee that had been heavily sandbagged.

Even armored, however, Humvees offer limited protection. While there were no reported deaths in attacks upon armored Humvees in the war, many passengers suffered injuries, and the vehicles themselves were often rendered unusable after suffering attacks from Iraqi insurgents.

The advanced technology of the coalition forces clearly helped to preserve coalition life, but at an unknown cost. For example, the Kevlar vests worn by soldiers proved highly effective at stopping enemy rounds and limiting the number of coalition deaths. However, the vests did nothing to protect the arms, legs, and faces of soldiers. The Walter Reed Military Hospital in Washington, D.C., became filled with amputees, many of whom were seriously injured while riding in unarmored Humvees. Although the soldiers survived their wounds, many remained bitter and fretted about their futures.

The problem of protecting Humvee passengers was not the only difficulty facing military planners. Even the heavily armored and technologically sophisticated Abrams tank showed it was not without its faults during Operation Iraqi Freedom.

Military officials found that the top and rear armor of the tanks were "susceptible to penetration."[49] One Abrams was disabled near Karbala when a rocket-propelled grenade entered the rear engine compartment. Another Abrams was put out of action in Baghdad when its external auxiliary power unit was set on fire by Iraqi rounds.

Asymmetric Attacks

Sometimes, there was no technology available that could possibly have aided coalition troops. On March 24, 2003, for example, a unit of Iraqi troops purportedly surrendered to U.S. forces. But the "surrender" was a ruse for an ambush. Thereafter, ground troops were especially wary and experienced stress, tension, and uncertainty that no level of technology could erase.

Similarly, coalition troops faced constant threats from irregular fighters—guerrilla warriors whose dress was indistinguishable from that of Iraqi civilians. Guerrillas driving small trucks outfitted with grenade launchers struck at coalition troops and sped away, and suicide bombers undertook deadly attacks at coalition checkpoints and other sites. Technology proved no match for such asymmetric attacks and further increased the stress levels of ground troops, whose job went from defeating Iraq's military to attempting to keep order as Iraq's political structure and infrastructure were rebuilt.

Technology allowed coalition forces to achieve a quick and decisive victory over an Iraqi foe that often was not even aware it had been detected. Sophisticated weapons systems and munitions, directed by highly accurate intelligence, allowed the coalition to achieve its military objectives with relatively few troops and with a low loss of coalition life. Nevertheless, the unique conditions of waging war in the desert, and of waging war against an ongoing insurgency, showed the limits of technological superiority.

★ Notes ★

Introduction: "Iraq Has Stockpiles of. . . Chemical . . . Agent"

1. Quoted in "Secretary Rumsfeld Interview—Bob Schieffer and David Martin," U.S. Department of Defense, March 23, 2003. www.defenselink.mil/news/Mar 2003/t03232003_t0323cbs.html.

2. George W. Bush, "President Bush Outlines Iraqi Threat," The White House, October 7, 2002. www.whitehouse.gov/news/releases/2002/10/20021007-8.html.

3. Quoted in Brad Knickerbocker, "Behind the Changing Rationales for War," *Christian Science Monitor,* June 13, 2003. www.globalpolicy.org/security/issues/iraq/unmovic/2003/0613rationales.htm.

4. George W. Bush, "President Bush Announces Major Combat Operations in Iraq Have Ended," The White House, May 1, 2003. www.whitehouse.gov/news/releases/2003/05/iraq/20030501-15.html.

Chapter 1: Naval Assets: Fire, and Comfort, from the Sea

5. Quoted in *Undersea Warfare,* "On Deployment?—Come as You Are," www.chinfo.navy.mil/navpalib/cno/n87/usw/issue_19/iraqifree-b.htm.

6. Quoted in Jeremy M. Vought "Bravo Company Tent Hospital Turns to Modern-Day M-A-S-H," U.S. Marine Corps, May 27, 2003. www.usmc.mil/marinelink/mcn2000nsf/lookupstoryref/2003 5278486.

7. Quoted in Vought, "Bravo Company Tent Hospital Turns to Modern-Day M-A-S-H."

8. Quoted in Vought, "Bravo Company Tent Hospital Turns to Modern-Day M-A-S-H."

9. Quoted in Loren Barnes, "Navy Hospital Jacksonville 'Devil Docs' Deploy," *Navy Newsstand,* February 13, 2004. www.news.navy.mil/search/display.asp?story_id=11849.

Chapter 2: Aircraft over Iraq: The Fixed-Wing Arsenal

10. Quoted in Chuck Roberts, "Airmen Fight to Help End the Regime of Saddam Hussein," *Airman,* May 2003. www.af.mil/news/airman/0503/oif.html.

11. Quoted in Harris Whitbeck, "War Stories: Donut in a Warthog," CNN, April 4, 2003. www.cnn.com/2003/WORLD/meast/04/04/sprj.irq.donut.

12. Quoted in U.S. National Guard, AmeriForce, www.reserve-nationalguard.com.

13. Quoted in Roberts, "Airmen Fight to Help End the Regime of Saddam Hussein."

Chapter 3: Helicopters in Iraq: "If They Move, We'll Go After Them"

14. Quoted in Todd S. Purdum, *A Time of Our Choosing: America's War in Iraq.* New York: Henry Holt, 2003, p. 190.
15. Quoted in Purdum, *A Time of Our Choosing,* p. 128.
16. Oliver L. North, *War Stories: Operation Iraqi Freedom.* Washington, DC: Regnery, 2003, p. 141.

Chapter 4: Fire from the Air: Shock and Awe

17. Quoted in Purdum, *A Time of Our Choosing,* p. 124.
18. Quoted in Kristina Barrett, "Building JDAMs for 'Shock and Awe,'" U.S. Air Forces in Europe, March 23, 2003. www.usafe.af.mil/news/news03/uns03182.htm
19. Quoted in Barrett, "Building JDAMs for 'Shock and Awe.'"
20. Quoted in April Gorenflo, "HST Strikes in Operation Iraqi Freedom," www.news.navy.mil/search/display.asp?story_id=6527.
21. Quoted in Douglas H. Stutz, "Inside the CAOC: Saving Civilian Lives with Collateral Damage Estimation," U.S. Air Force. www.af.mil/news/story.asp?storyID=4170367.
22. Quoted in Stutz, "Inside the CAOC."
23. Quoted in Stutz, "Inside the CAOC."

24. Quoted in Bob Jensen, "Weather Forecasters Aid Mission Planning," *Air Force Link.* www.af.mil/news/story.asp?storyID=3190353.
25. Quoted in Bob Jensen, "Planners Take Full Advantage of Weather," Inside the CAOC: Weather, Air Tactics, May 2003. www.barksdale.af.mil/8af/news/May03.pdf.

Chapter 5: Ground War Weapons: "The Baghdad Urban Renewal Project"

26. Quoted in U.S. Army Soldier Systems Center Public Affairs Office, "New Fibers Could Lighten Body Armor," *RDECOM Magazine,* January 2004. www.rdecom.army.mil/rdemagazine/200401/itl_nsc_armor.html.
27. Quoted in North, *War Stories,* p. 42.
28. Quoted in North, *War Stories,* p. 39.

Chapter 6: Surveillance

29. Quoted in T.A. Heppenheimer, *Countdown: A History of Space Flight.* New York: John Wiley & Sons, 1997, p. 126.
30. Quoted in Dan Caterinicchia, "JSTARS Keeps Eye on Enemy," *Federal Computer Week,* April 2, 2003. www.fcw.com/fcw/articles/2003/Middle_East/web-jstars-04-02-03.asp.
31. Quoted in Brian Orban, "Inside the CAOC: Targeteering," *Air Force Link,* www.af.mil/news/airman/1003/target.html.
32. Quoted in Roberts, "Airmen Fight to Help End the Regime of Saddam Hussein."

33. Quoted in Roberts, "Airmen Fight to Help End the Regime of Saddam Hussein."

Chapter 7 Psychological Operations: "Your Cause Is Lost"

34. Wesley K. Clark, *Winning Modern Wars: Iraq, Terrorism, and the American Empire.* New York: Public Affairs, 2003, p. 12.
35. Quoted in *Radio Netherlands.* "Psychological Warfare Against Iraq," www.rnw.nl/realradio/features/html/iraq-psywar.html.
36. Quoted in Jeff Glasser, "Psychological Operations: Getting the U.S. Message to Iraqis," *U.S. News & World Report,* March 22, 2003. www.usnews.com/usnews/news/iraq/articles/qatar030321.html.
37. Quoted in Herbert A. Friedman, "Psychological Operations in Iraq: No-FIy Zone Warning Leaflets to Iraq, 2002–2003," *PsyWar.Org,* http://psyborg.co.uk/noflyzone.php.
38. Quoted in Purdum, *A Time of Our Choosing,* p. 98.
39. Quoted in Purdum, *A Time of Our Choosing,* p. 177.
40. Quoted in Purdum, *A Time of Our Choosing,* p. 177.
41. Quoted in Dan Caterinicchia "DOD Confirms Iraq E-mail Campaign," *Federal Computer Week,* January 16, 2003. www.fcw.com/fcw/articles/2003/0113/web-iraq-01-16-03.asp.
42. Quoted in Matthew French, "DOD Aims Psy-Ops at Iraqi Officers," *Federal Computer Week,* March 24, 2003. www.fcw.com/fcw/articles/2003/0317/web-psyops-03-21-03.asp.
43. Quoted in Friedman, "Psychological Operations in Iraq."
44. Quoted in Friedman, "Psychological Operations in Iraq."
45. Clark, *Winning Modern Wars,* p. 36.
46. Quoted in Purdum, *A Time of Our Choosing,* p. 205.
47. North, *War Stories,* p. 161.

Chapter 8: The Limits of Technological Superiority

48. Quoted in Tara Copp and Jessica Wehrman, "American Troops Forced to Buy Own Wartime Gear," *Scripps Howard News Service,* September 11, 2003. www.globalsecurity.org/org/news/2003/030911-boots01.html.
49. Quoted in Tim Ripley, "Abrams Tank Showed 'Vulnerability' in Iraq," *Jane's Defence Weekly,* June 20, 2003. www.janes.com/regional_news/americas/news/jdw/jdw030620_1_n.shtml.

★ For Further Reading ★

Books

Leila Merrell Foster, *Iraq: Enchantment of the World*. New York: Childrens, 1998. A broad look at Iraq, including the country's rich culture, history, and natural resources.

John Hamilton, *Weapons of War: A Pictorial History of the Past One Thousand Years*. Edina, MN: ABDO & Daughters, 2002. A rich and colorful history of military weaponry, with an overview of modern weapons of war.

Zachary Kent, *The Persian Gulf War: "Mother of All Battles."* Hillside, NJ: Enslow, 1994. An examination of the 1991 Persian Gulf War, with a discussion of weapons systems that were also used in the 2003 Iraq War.

Web Sites

Global Policy Forum (www.globalpolicy.org). This site presents a broad range of articles and editorials examining the nation's involvement in and conduct of war in Iraq.

Global Security.Org (www.globalsecurity. org). A vast and comprehensive Web site with a host of articles relating to the Iraq War and the weapons used to wage it.

Jane's Defence Weekly (www.janes.com). An authoritative resource on military weaponry with updates on weapons utilized during the Iraq War.

PsyWar.Org (www.psyborg.co.uk). An intriguing Web site devoted to psychological warfare.

U.S. Army Soldier Systems Center (www. rdecom.army.mil). An excellent resource for information relating to the development of improved soldier safety equipment.

U.S. Central Command (www.centcom.mil) A comprehensive source of articles, transcripts, and press releases from the Iraq War command center.

U.S. Department of Defense (www.defense link.mil) The official Department of Defense Web site contains links to all aspects of the U.S. military operation in Iraq, including weaponry.

☆ Works Consulted ☆

Books

Wesley K. Clark, *Winning Modern Wars: Iraq, Terrorism, and the American Empire.* New York: Public Affairs, 2003. The former NATO commander and Iraq War analyst provides an intriguing look at the strategies utilized during the Iraq War.

T.A. Heppenheimer, *Countdown: A History of Space Flight.* New York: John Wiley & Sons, 1997. An engaging examination of the space race, including Cold War fears that domination of space by the Soviet Union could jeopardize the United States.

Oliver L. North, *War Stories: Operation Iraqi Freedom.* Washington, DC: Regnery, 2003. An interesting glimpse of the Iraq War from the perspective of a former marine lieutenant colonel and White House aide who played a key role in the Iran-Contra affair of the 1980s and who served as an embedded correspondent in the Iraq War.

Kenneth M. Pollack, *The Threatening Storm: The Case for Invading Iraq.* New York: Random House, 2002. A recognized expert on the Middle East examines the issues faced by the U.S. government as leaders prepared for war in Iraq.

Todd S. Purdum, *A Time of Our Choosing: America's War in Iraq.* New York: Henry Holt, 2003. A comprehensive look at the Iraq War, including what it was like for soldiers on the ground.

Christopher Scheer, Robert Scheer, and Lakshmi Chandhry, *The Five Biggest Lies Bush Told Us About Iraq.* New York: Akashic and Seven Stories, 2003. Opponents of the Bush administration's Iraq policy detail complaints about the nation's decision to invade Iraq.

Internet Sources

John Abizaid, Vincent Brooks, and Peter Wall, "CENTCOM Operation Iraqi Freedom Briefing," Briefing Transcript, March 23, 2003. www.centcom.mil/CENTCOMNews/Transcripts/20030323a.htm.

Loren Barnes, "Navy Hospital Jacksonville 'Devil Docs' Deploy," *Navy Newstand,* February 13, 2004. www.news.navy.mil/search/display.asp?story_id=11849.

Kristina Barrett, "Building JDAMs for 'Shock and Awe,'" U.S. Air Forces in Europe, March 23, 2003. www.usafe.af.mil/news/news03 /uns03182.htm.

George W. Bush, "President Bush Announces Major Combat Operations in Iraq Have Ended," The White House,

May 1, 2003. www.whitehouse.gov/news/releases/2003/05/iraq/20030501-15.html.

———, "President Bush Outlines Iraqi Threat," The White House, October 7, 2002. www.whitehouse.gov/news/releases/2002/10/20021007-8.html.

Dan Caterinicchia, "DOD Confirms Iraq E-mail Campaign," *Federal Computer Week,* January 16, 2003. www.fcw.com/fcw/articles/2003/0113/web-iraq-01-16-03.asp.

———, "JSTARS Keeps Eye on Enemy," *Federal Computer Week,* April 2, 2003. www.fcw.com/fcw/articles/2003/Middle_East/web-jstars-04-02-03.asp.

Tara Copp and Jessica Wehrman, "American Troops Forced to Buy Own Wartime Gear," *Scripps Howard News Service,* September 11, 2003. www.globalsecurity.org/org/news/2003/030911-boots01.html.

Department of Defense, "Secretary Rumsfeld and General Myers News Briefing," News Transcript, February 10, 2004. www.defenselink.mil/transcripts/2004/tr20040210-0436.html.

Jonathan Franklin, "The War According to David Hackworth," Common Dreams News Center, August 5, 2003. www.commondreams.org/views03/0805-09.htm.

Matthew French, "DOD Aims Psy-Ops at Iraqi Officers," *Federal Computer Week,* March 24, 2003. www.fcw.com/fcw/articles/2003/0317/web-psyops-03-21-03.asp.

Herbert A. Friedman, "Psychological Operations in Iraq: No-Fly Zone Warning Leaflets to Iraq, 2002–2003," *PsyWar.Org,* http://psyborg.c.uk/noflyzone.php.

Jeff Glasser, "Psychological Operations: Getting the U.S. Message to Iraqis," *U.S. News & World Report,* March 22, 2003. www.usnews.com/usnews/news/iraq/articles/qatar030321.hmtl.

Steve Goose, "Cluster Munitions: Toward a Global Solution," *Human Rights Watch,* January 2004. www.hrw.org/wr2k4/12.htm.

April Gorenflo, "HST Strikes in Operation Iraqi Freedom," www.news.navy.mil/search/display.asp?story_id=6527.

Bob Jensen, "Planners Take Full Advantage of Weather," Inside the CAOC: Weather, Air Tactics, May 2003. www.barksdale.af.mil/8af/news/May03.pdf.

———, "Theater Frequency Management Organizes Airwaves," *Air Force Link,* April 16, 2003. www.af.mil/news/story.asp?storyID=416033.

———, "Weather Forecasters Aid Mission Planning," Air Force Link, www.af.mil/news/story.asp?StoryID=3190353.

Brad Knickerbocker, "Behind the Changing Rationales for War," *Christian Science Monitor,* June 13, 2003. www.globalpolicy.org/security/issues/iraq/unmovic/2003/0613rationales.htm.

NAVAIR China Lake Public Affairs, "NAVAIR Designs, Builds More Potent Hellfire Warhead," *Navy Newsstand,* July 23, 2003. www.news.navy.mil/search/display.asp?story_id=8625.

Brian Orban, "Inside the CAOC: Targeteering," *Air Force Link,* www.af.mil/news/airman/1003/target.html.

Mark O. Piggott, "Three Sub Commanders Awarded Bronze Star for OIF," *Navy Newsstand*, December 3, 2003. www.news.navy.mil/search/display.asp?story_id=10876.

Radio Netherlands, "Psychological Warfare Against Iraq," www.rnw.nl/realradio/features/html/iraq-psywar.html.

Tim Ripley, "Abrams Tank Showed 'Vulnerability' in Iraq," *Jane's Defence Weekly,* June 20, 2003. www.janes.com/regional_news/americas/news/jdw/dw030620_1_n.shtml.

Chuck Roberts, "Airmen Fight to Help End the Regime of Saddam Hussein," *Airman,* May 2003. www.af.mil/news/airman/0503/oif.html.

Sonya Ross and Chris Tomlinson, "View from Above: The Air War," CBS News.com, March 28, 2003. www.cbsnews.com/stories/2003/03/28/iraq/main546496.shtml.

"Secretary Rumsfeld Interview—Bob Schieffer and David Martin," U.S. Department of Defense, March 23, 2003. www.defenselink.mil/news/Mar2003/t03232003_t0323cbs.html.

Douglas H. Stutz, "Inside the CAOC: Saving Civilian Lives with Collateral Damage Estimation," U.S. Air Force, www.af.mil/news/story.asp?storyID=4170367.

——— "Logistical Thinking from the Ground to Air," U.S. Marine Corps, April 3, 2003. www.usmc.mil/marinelink/mcn2000.nsf.

Undersea Warfare, "On Deployment?—Come as You Are," www.chinfo.navy.mil/navpalib/cno/n87/usw/issue_19/iraqifree_b.htm.

U.S. Army Soldier Systems Center Public Affairs Office, "New Fibers Could Lighten Body Armor," *RDECOM Magazine,* January 2004. www.rdecom.army.mil/rdemagazine/200401/itl_nsc_armor.html.

U.S. National Guard, AmeriForce, www.reserve-nationalguard.com.

Jeremy M. Vought, "Bravo Company Tent Hospital Turns to Modern-Day M-A-S-H," U.S. Marine Corps, May 27, 2003. www. usmc.mil/marinelink/mcn2000.nsf/lookupstoryref/20035278486.

Harris Whitbeck, "War Stories: Donut in a Warthog," CNN, April 4, 2003. www.cnn.com/2003/WORLD/meast/04/04/sprj.irq.donut.

★ Index ★

A10/OA-10 Thunderbolt II (Warthog), 28, 31–32

Abizaid, John, 66

Abraham Lincoln (ship), 22

Abrams tanks, 63–66, 95–96

AC-130H/U gunships, 30–31

Advanced K-11 satellite, 69

Afghanistan, U.S. invasion of, 11

AH-1W Super Cobra helicopters, 36–38

airborne warning and control system (AWACS), 32–33

aircraft
    cargo, 34–35
    drones, 69
    frequency management of, 32
    navigation systems, 29
    reconnaissance, 69, 71–76
    refueling, 33–34
    support, 32–34
    of U.S. Navy/Marines, 29–30
    weather conditions and, 55–56
    see also helicopters; *and specific aircraft*

Apache helicopters, 38–41

armor, protective, 57–59, 91

asymmetric attacks, 96

AWACS (airborne warning and control system), 32–33

B-2 Spirit, 26–27

B-52 Stratofortress, 25–26

Ball, Daniel, 41

Black Hawk helicopters, 41–42

BLU-82 bomb, 51–52

body armor, 57–59, 91

bombs
    basics of, 48
    smart, 13, 48, 51
    targeting, 53–55
    see also specific bombs

Bradley fighting vehicles, 61–63

Bronze Star, 22

Bush, George W.
    justifications for war by, 12
    on success of Operation Iraqi Freedom, 13
    on threat posed by Iraq, 11

Butler, Darryl M., 95

C-17s, 35

cargo aircraft, 34–35

cargo ships, 14–16

CH-46 helicopters, 43–44

CH-47 Chinook helicopters, 42–43

chemical protection suits, 59

Cheyenne (ship), 21–22

Clark, Wesley K., 77–78, 85

Clothier, Cathy, 33

CLP, 93

cluster bombs, 53

Cobra Ball aircraft, 73

Cobra helicopters, 36–38

collateral damage, 20, 48, 53–55

combat gear, 59–60, 91

Combined Forces Air Component
   Command (CFACC), 32

Comfort (ship), 22–24

communication problems, 92–93

Cuniff, Philip, 59

Daisy Cutters, 51–52

decapitation strikes, failed, 87–89

depleted uranium, 63–65

Devil Docs, 23–24

Diven, Chuck, 33

dolphins, mine-sweeping, 17–18

Doty, Charles, 21–22

Dowdy, Robert, 94

drones, 69

E-3 Sentry, 32–33

EC-130 Commando Solo, 77, 78, 79

e-mail campaign, 79–81

enemy, demoralizing, 75, 78–79

   see also psychological operations

equipment

   malfunctioning, 93

   transport of, 14–16

Extenders, 34

F-15E Strike Eagle, 27, 29

F/A-18 Hornet, 30

Fabozzi, Joseph, 91

Fahlbusch, Fred, 55, 56

fast-sealift ships, 15

Feringa, Matt, 37

507th Maintenance Company, 93–94

Flourney, Michele, 28

Frake, William J., 22

France, 12

frequency management, 32

Frickey, Douglas, 53–54, 55

friendly fire, 30

Garrett, Patrick, 92

Geneva Convention, 22

Germany, 12

Global Hawks, 75–76

global positioning system (GPS), 67,
   68–69, 90

Gonzalez, Adam, 72

Goose, Steve, 53

gravity bombs, 48

grenades, 60–61

ground war

   success of, 57

   weaponry, 57–66

   see also soldiers

guerrilla fighters, 96

Gulf War (1991), 12–13, 16

guns, 60–61, 63

Hackworth, David C., 92

Hamrick, Sonya M., 24

helicopters, basics of, 37

   see also specific helicopters

Hellfire missiles, 47, 52

helmets, 58, 59

Hornet, 30

Human Rights Watch, 53

Humvees, 63, 93–95

Hussein, Qusay, 45

Hussein, Saddam
  danger posed by, 11–12
  failed strikes against, 87–89

Hussein, Uday, 45

Information Radio, 78

information war. *See* psychological
  operations

intelligence failures, 89

Iraq
  threat posed by, 11
  WMDs possessed by, 11–12, 89

Iraqi navy, 14, 16

Iraq War
  media access during, 85
  opposition to, 12
  U.S. case for, 12
  U.S. strategy for, 28

Jensen, Bob, 32

Johnson, Lyndon B., 67–68

joint directional attack munitions
  (JDAMs), 49–51

Joint Venture (boat), 19

JSTARS, 70–71

KC-10 Extenders, 34

KC-135 Stratotankers, 33–34

large, medium speed roll-on/roll-off
  ships (LMSR), 14–15

laser-guided bombs, 51

leaflet drops, 81–82, 85

logistics, of air campaign, 35

long-range acoustic devices, 66

Lynch, Jessica, 94

M-16 rifles, 60

M242 chain guns, 61

M4 carbines, 60, 93

M67 fragmentation grenades, 60–61

Marine Mammal System, 17

maritime prepositioning ships, 14

Mark V boats, 19

massive ordance air-blast (MOAB)
  bomb, 52, 84–85

Maverick missiles, 52–53, 54

medical support, 22–24

Military Sealift Command, 15

MILSTAR satellite, 69–70

mine-clearing operations, 16–18

missiles. *See specific missiles*

munitions. *See* bombs; weaponry

MW56 guns, 63

Naval Air Systems Command (NAVAIR),
  47

navigation systems, 29

Navstar, 68

night-vision goggles, 59–60

nonlethal weapons, 66

North, Oliver L., 44, 66, 86

oil industry, 82

Olson, Thomas A., 24

101st Airborne Division (Screaming
  Eagles), 45

Operation Desert Storm, 12–13
Operation Iraqi Freedom. See Iraq War
outer space, 67–68

Patriot missile air defense system, 61
Pave Hawk helicopters, 42, 95
Pave Low helicopters, 44–45
Persian Gulf War (1991), 12–13, 14, 16
personal armor system, ground troops
  (PASGT), 58
Piestewa, Lori Ann, 93
Pirkey, Jonathan, 35
planes. See aircraft
Poole, Kevin R., 24
Potratz, Mike, 49, 50
Powell, Colin, 12
precision munitions, 46, 48
Predator, 73–75
prisoners of war (POWs), medical
  treatment of, 22–24
protective armor, 57–59, 91
psychological operations
  bullhorn campaigns, 78–79
  conducted by Iraq, 85–86
  on Internet, 79–81
  leaflets, 81–82, 85
  radio broadcasts, 77–78
  shock-and-awe campaign, 82, 84–85
  surrender urged during, 81–82
  television broadcasts, 81

al Qaeda, 11
Quintrall, Mick, 70–71

radar systems, 70–71

radio broadcasts, 77–78
Radio Tikrit, 78
RC-135V/2 Rivet Joint, 71–72
REMUS, 17
rifles, 60–61
rigid-hull inflatable boats (RHIBs), 19
Rivet Joint, 71–72
Ross, Sonya, 28
Rumsfeld, Donald, 11, 54–55, 81

al-Sahaf, Saeed, 84, 86
Sanderson, Jeffrey Randall, 79
sand flies, 90
sandstorms, 89–90
satellites
  Advanced K-11, 69
  GPS, 68–69
  importance of, 69–70
  MILSTAR, 69–70
  uses of, 67
Screaming Eagles. See 101st Airborne
  Division
Sea Hawk helicopters, 42
SEALS, 16, 18–19
Sentell, John, 24
September 11, 2001, 11
Sewell, Donald, 47
Sherman, William Tecumseh, 75
shock-and-awe campaign, 46, 48, 82,
  84–85
Simmons, Randy, 26
smart weapons
  advantages of, 13
  laser-guided, 51
  numbers of, used, 48, 50

Smith, Darrell, 64
soldiers
  combat gear for, 59–60
  confidence of, 66
  poorly supplied, 90–92
  protective armor for, 57–59
Soviet Union, 67
space, importance of, 67–68
space-based systems, 68–70
stealth aircraft, 26–27
strategic strikes, speed of, 83
Stratotankers, 33–34
Strike Eagle, 27, 29
Stutz, Douglas, 35
submarines, 21–22
Sun-tzu, 46
super bombs, 51–52
supply problems, 90–92
surveillance tools
  JSTARS, 70–71
  reconnaissance aircraft, 69, 71–76
  satellites, 67–70
  space-based systems, 68–70

Taliban, 11
targets, identifying, 72
technological superiority, limits of,
  87–96
television broadcasts, 81
Tomahawk missiles, 19–22
Tomlinson, Chris, 28
TOW antitank missile system, 61–62
Trzaskoma, Traz, 74

UH-1 helicopter (Huey), 36, 38

UH-60 Black Hawk helicopter, 41–42
Ullman, Harlan K., 46
Umm Qasr, 16–18
United States
  case for Iraq War by, 12
  claims by, of Iraq WMDs, 11–12
unmanned aerial vehicles (UAVs), 72–76
Upton, Rob, 51
uranium, depleted, 63–65
U.S. Air Force, superiority of, 25
U.S. intelligence failures, 89
U.S. Marines, 29–30
U.S. Navy
  aircraft of, 29–30
  medical support by, 22–24
  mine-clearing operations of, 16–18
  SEALS, 16, 18–19
  Tomahawk missiles launched by,
    19–22
  transport of material by, 14–16

vehicles
  Abrams tanks, 63–66
  Bradley fighting vehicles, 61–63
  Humvees, 63, 93–95
  unarmored, 93–95
vests, 58, 59
Vietnam War, 36
Voice of the Gulf, 77–78

war matériel, transport of, 14–16
war on terrorism, 11
Warthogs, 28, 31–32
weaponry
  grenades, 60–61

ground, 57–66
improving, 47
malfunctioning, 93
MW56 guns, 63
nonlethal, 66
rifles, 60–61
see also bombs; missiles

weapons of mass destruction (WMDs)
  lack of, 89
  possessed by Iraq, 11–12
weather forecasting, 55–56
weather problems, 89–90

Zimmermann, John C., 32

★ Picture Credits ★

Cover: Shawn Baldwin/EPA/Landov
© AP Wide World, 80
Peter Andrews/Reuters/Landov, 28
Yannis Behrakis/Reuters/Landov, 38
Ken Bergmann/Bloomberg News/Landov, 79
Bloomberg News/Landov, 27, 49
Russell Boyle/Reuters/Landov, 54
EPA/Landov, 68
© George Hall/CORBIS, 44
Paul Hanna/Reuters/Landov, 83
Paul Jarrett/EPA/Landov, 43
© David Leeson/Dallas Morning News/CORBIS, 62
© Benjamin Lowy/CORBIS, 58

MAI/Landov, 47
Reuters/Cedric H. Rudisill/USAF/Handout/Landov, 88
© Reuters/CORBIS, 23
Reuters/Kai Pfaffenbach/Landov, 91, 94
Reuters/Landov, 21, 29, 31, 41, 50, 84
Reuters/Larry Downing/Landov, 12
Reuters/Royal Navy/Handout/Landov, 17
Reuters/USAF/Handout/Landov, 26
© Damir Sagolj/Reuters/CORBIS, 60
© Leif Skoogfors/CORBIS, 18
Goran Tomasevic/Reuters/Landov, 39
UPI/Landov, 71, 74
UPI/Suzanne M. Jenkins/Air Force/Landov, 34

★ About the Author ★

Geoffrey A. Campbell is a freelance writer in Fort Worth, Texas. Campbell holds a journalism degree from the University of Missouri. His work frequently appears in the *Fort Worth Star-Telegram,* for which he writes book reviews, articles for the life section, and opinion-editorial pieces. He also writes for *World Book Yearbook,* contributing articles relating to the U.S. government. He has written six previous titles for Lucent Books. For relaxation, Campbell is active as a youth sports coach and plays hardball in the Fort Worth Men's Senior Baseball League.

3|05